Son of the Headmaster at R(
Allen Leeds was from his earl
life in agriculture – he now lives on a Herefordshire fruit farm,
and the years in between are largely the subject of this book.

After completing a Diploma course at Wye college in Kent
in 1938, he accepted a Colonial Office post in the Department
of Agriculture in West Africa and set sail from Liverpool to
another world.

When war broke out Allen joined the Gold Coast Regiment
which was part of the Royal West African Frontier Force. The
book gives thrilling descriptions of warfare in the wild
thornbush country on the Abyssinian and Somaliland borders,
with big game always in evidence. Later the hard fought battle
of Uaddara in Southern Abyssinia is covered, with Addis Ababa
being reached in June 1940.

After two and a half years in the army, the need for increased
food production necessitated a return to civilian life. Much of
Allen's time in the Gold Coast concerned the cocoa industry
and he was in time promoted to the post of Assistant Director
of Agriculture in charge of cocoa agronomy, and disease control
in particular. The chapters that deal with this work give an
insight into the years when the British Empire helped to
develop modern methods of Agriculture on the African
continent.

The book contains an account of the transition of the Gold
Coast to Ghana, with descriptions of the life-style of expatriates
and others in what was then aptly known as the "White Man's
Grave." Truly, the author gives his readers a glimpse of a world
that is indeed, "Long Ago and Far Away".

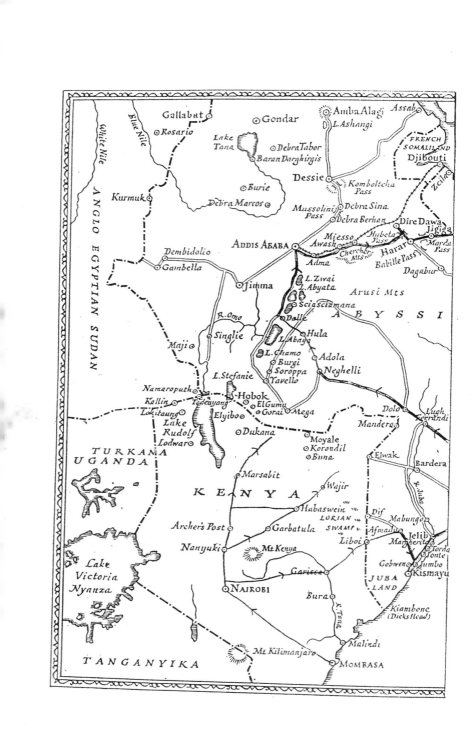

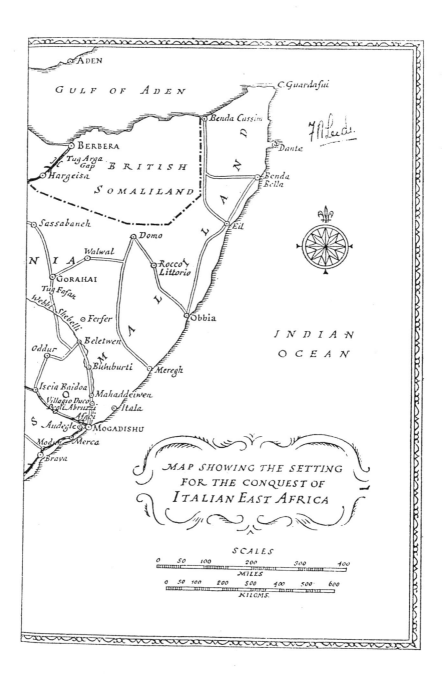

MAP SHOWING THE SETTING
FOR THE CONQUEST OF
ITALIAN EAST AFRICA

For when the One Great Scorer comes
to mark against your name,
He writes – not that you won or lost –
but how you played the Game

(Grantland Rice)

LONG AGO AND FAR AWAY

Gold Coast Days
1939–1958

Allen Leeds

A Square One Publication

First published in 1998 by
Square One Publications,
The Tudor House
Upton upon Severn
Worcestershire WR8 0HT

ISBN 1 899955 29 1

A British Library Cataloguing in Data
is available for this title

*Typeset in Times New Roman 11 on 13 by
Avon Dataset Ltd, Bidford-on-Avon, Warwickshire
Printed by Antony Rowe Ltd, Chippenham, Wiltshire*

Contents

Maps

List of Illustrations

Acknowledgements

I should like to thanks the following who read the text and gave their advice:

Eric Lanning – Military matters

Hilary Leeds – my sister

Harry Pierrepoint – formerly in the Field Ambulance

Roy Silverlock – An Agricultural colleague

To Barbara

THE GOLD COAST

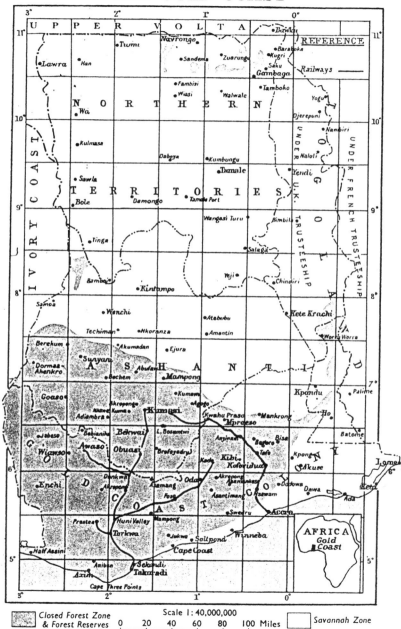

1

Introduction

I was born in 1916 at Hanley Castle, a small village in Worcestershire, my father being the head master of the local grammar school. In 1921 we moved to Ross-on-Wye where he took over a similar position.

From a very early age it was my ambition to become a farmer. Even at the age of eight, I surprised everyone by subscribing to such weeklies at the Farmer and Stock-breeder, the Feathered World and the Smallholder and Gardener! My idea of an entertaining morning was to attend the local cattle market.

Apart from my interests in agriculture, I was also a keen naturalist, particularly in the fields of entomology and ornithology. I was a keen collector of moths and butterflies and also birds' eggs, a hobby not frowned upon in those days.

I attended Bromsgrove School from 1929 to 1934 and though prominent in the first Rugby XV and a house monitor, my academic achievements were far from brilliant. After leaving Bromsgrove I became a farm pupil at Knightwick Manor, a large mixed farm in Worcestershire owned by a well-known local farmer, John Walker. I will only mention in passing that the farm was a large mixed one, some 500 acres in extent and set in lovely countryside. It featured – apart from the usual arable crops – hops, Hereford cattle and miscellaneous fruit orchards including cherries.

It was characteristic of those days that the farm employed as many as 20 or 30 full-time workers, though it must be said that the minimum pay was as low as 30 shillings a week. There were waggoners, stockmen and general farm workers, a foreman, a blacksmith, a shepherd and several young lads gaining experience. One surprise was that the farm supported two full-time rabbit catchers! Living in with the family as I did, I got a little tired of rabbit being so frequently on the menu. Rabbit for lunch and supper was not too bad, but it became a bit too much when it started appearing for breakfast as well!

Towards the end of my year at Knightwick, it became clear that even in those far off days, substantial capital was required to start a farm on one's own. Accordingly it was decided that I should take a three-year agricultural diploma course at Wye College in Kent. I was at Wye from 1935 to 1938 where I worked and played hard. This was before the present days of coeducation and degree courses only and it might be said that a good time was had by all.

After leaving Wye with my diploma, I gave up the idea of looking for a job in agriculture in the United Kingdom and instead sought employment overseas. Eventually I accepted the post of Inspector of Produce in the Gold Coast under the Colonial Office which carried at that time an annual salary of £450.

Like most newly appointed colonial officers, I travelled to London to purchase my requirements for my first eighteen months tour on the West Coast of Africa. Needless to say I visited the then well-known emporium of Griffith McAllister in Warwick Street just behind the Regent Palace Hotel. Here one could buy every possible requirement for life in the tropics.

My purchases included bush shirts, shorts, palm beach suits, solar topees, camp equipment, crockery, cutlery and silver, glasses, Tilley lamps, etc., etc. I recollect that the bill for the complete outfit was in the region of £65, a pittance by modern standards. All was delivered to the ship at Liverpool in strongly made metal uniform trunks, also of course supplied by Griffith McAllister.

From a neighbour in Ross who had previously been invalided from Nigeria, I also acquired a metal hat box to store the topees in, a camp bed and a large metal camp bath, which with its wicker lining and locking top could also be used as a holdall for clothes. It was not many years previous to this that government officers took out 'chop boxes' of tinned provisions sufficient to last out their tour of duty.

2

The Voyage Out

I was due to sail from Liverpool for West Africa at the end of April 1939 on the Elder Dempster mail ship, the *Accra*. My parents had come up to see me off and we stayed the night at the Stork Hotel. I have always wondered since whether there was something odd about the Stork as when I mentioned its name to Liverpudlians they tended to laugh. I never discovered the reason for this, though perhaps it had a rather shady reputation!

Rather surprisingly, right up to several years after the war, there were only two other respectable hotels in Liverpool, the nice middle class hotel the Exchange, which I used on subsequent visits and the more flashy Adelphi where I only stayed once. When returning from leave I found it necessary to spend one or more nights in Liverpool as I usually had a new car to load on the ship.

In those far off days it was a great experience to take a ride on the overhead railway which followed the line of the docks for several miles. There one could see dozens of ocean going ships loading and discharging their cargos. Now the railway has gone, the ships are many fewer in number and other uses have been found for the many warehouses. I am glad to say, however, that the sight of the Liver birds on their tall building still greets the nostalgic eye of the old Coaster returning from leave in West Africa. Readers may think it a little presumptuous of me to use the term 'Coaster', whether old or not, as synonymous with workers from the West Coast of Africa, but they were freely known as such in Liverpool in those days.

After a particularly stormy crossing of the Bay of Biscay, we arrived three days later at Madeira. Not a lot was seen of Funchal, the capital, however, as our arrival was at night and our stay for a few hours only. The sight of Madeira's shoreline brilliantly lit up by myriad lights was not easily forgotten. Twenty four hours later an equally short visit and trip ashore was made at Las Palmas, the main city of Gran Canaria in the Canary Island. The streets and sights of this large metropolis became much more familiar on later visits.

After Las Palmas the long haul down the West African coast commenced. On the morning following our shore trip, we woke to cloudless blue skies and what was not always so usual, a sea like the proverbial mill pond. Despite this, however, the ship maintained a steady though not uncomfortable roll. We soon made the acquaintance of 'Smokes', our bar room steward, while 'Decks' allocated us to our deck chairs for the duration of the voyage.

For the next ten days or so the voyage took up a quiet but never boring routine. Meals were lavish and the bars and lounges were well patronised by the hard drinking Coasters. It may come as a surprise to many that the first opening of the bar was at 7.30 a.m. before breakfast, and there were usually as many people there then, drinking Brandy Gingers and cold lagers, as could be found later in the day! Dressing for dinner was of course essential for us first class passengers, and in those days dress ties were meant to be tied and not worn ready made up. With the arrival of the tropics white mess jackets, often referred to as 'bum freezers' replaced the black dinner jackets. En suite baths were not then normal in cabins, and cabin stewards passed baths for individual passengers by rota every evening before dinner.

As on most other ships, sweeps and auctions, usually to do

with the length of the ship's run were daily features, as were the normal deck games. A particularly vicious game in which I was pressed to participate was deck cricket – The Gold Coast versus Nigeria. Almost obligatory before lunch was a simple poker game called 'Freeze Out', usually played for drinks. Both Liar and Poker dice were popular. After leaving the Canaries, flying fish made their first appearance, as did schools of porpoises. Bird life was confined to odd shearwaters mysteriously skimming over the waves miles out to sea. Sometimes we saw flotillas of Portuguese Men of War close to the ship – jellyfish with a very unpleasant sting.

Cabins were reasonably well appointed but there was no air conditioning, and relative coolness could only be obtained with the use of small electric fans, open port holes and wind scoops. At night the heavens were aglitter with innumerable stars, and

Diving for Pennies, Sierra Leone

6

when we obtained our first glimpse of the Southern Cross and the sight of the Plough 'upside down', we knew we were really in the tropics.

We did not go ashore at Bathurst in the Gambia, as we again arrived at night, but much more interesting was Freetown, the capital of Sierra Leone. Ships anchored in the outer harbour, where they were greeted by the occupants of numerous canoes prepared to dive for pennies thrown by the passengers. Their leader was an imposing African called Charlie Brown, who had first to doff his top hat before diving.

The first sights of the shores of Africa impressed me by the intense greenness of the landscape – quite a different green from the greenness of Europe, a bright emerald and viridescent green. It was very hot and sticky ashore in Freetown, but I was excited by the milling crowds of brightly dressed natives going about their business, even as far as the swarms of beggars, some badly handicapped, who surrounded us at times. A visit was made to the Bristol Hotel, made famous in a novel of Graham Greene's. It hardly came into the category of one of the world's finest hotels, and will no doubt continue to be better known for its cockroaches. I saw for the first time vultures sitting around ready for anything that might turn up, and there were a lot of kites flying about together with those aerial pirates, the frigate birds.

Some two weeks after leaving Liverpool we arrived at the fine Gold Coast port of Takoradi, where I expected to disembark. However, I instead received instructions to go on to Accra, another day's run along the coast.

Accra was and still is a surf port, and we anchored about a mile off the shore. All cargo for Accra had to be loaded into canoes, and we passengers who were to go ashore were deposited overboard two at a time in what was referred to as a 'mammy chair', and from there to the shore by canoe. The most exciting part was perhaps the last few yards to the shore with the canoe boys paddling furiously through the heavy surf, and with other boys carrying us bodily the last few yards. I was met on the shore by a member of the Agricultural Department who organised the passage of my loads through Customs. Meantime, the *Accra* left to sail on to Lagos and Calabar in Nigeria before commencing the return trip to the United Kingdom.

Elder Dempster Line
Mail ship Accra

3

Assuansi. May to August, 1939

On disembarkation, I spent two or three days in Accra, staying in the government rest house and being entertained to meals by various members of the Agricultural Department. This was an introduction to the hospitality always evident among European Coasters and obligatory where one's own department was concerned. In Accra I recruited a Nigerian cook named Hambo at the princely salary of £3 a month. Dusk to dark in the tropics takes only a few minutes, and as the Gold Coast is nearly on the equator, the period stays reasonably static throughout the year at about 6.30 p.m. The first evening in Accra, however, took me rather unawares when the dusk was heralded by a sudden cacophony of sound from the resident crickets and cicadas. Subsequently this chorus became so familiar as to pass quite unnoticed. Later in the night fruit bats in the neem trees kept up their monotonous calling.

One of my hosts in Accra took me to a well-known Syrian store to obtain supplies of provisions etc. for taking up country. The corpulent and prosperous Mr Bikhazi was, of course, delighted to open up a new account. Apart from the usual day-to-day groceries, my purchases included such 'essentials' as a case of Langs Liqueur Whisky and another of Accra Beer. Accra, incidentally, supported its own brewery.

A large government lorry was laid on for me to take, with Hambo, all my various loads to my first station, Assuansi. The route followed the coast road, some 80 miles to Cape Coast and then some 20 miles inland. Assuansi was the agricultural station for the Central Province, and at that time was largely devoted to the interests of citrus cultivation. Emphasis was given to a local lime industry which had been promoted by the firm of Rose's and who had two factories in the neighbourhood, at Abakrampa and Asebu.

At that time the Central Province was run by a senior Agricultural Officer, name of Scott, and he was also stationed at Assuansi and had his wife out at the time. I took over after about a week from a young man called 'Basher' Hughes, who was about to go on leave after completing his first tour. In actual fact he was no 'Basher' and I well remember him recounting to me with bated breath the advice he had received from a very formidable Assistant Director of Agriculture, named Wingate: 'Hughes, you must always have available in your bungalow for the unexpected visitor a bottle of whisky, a bottle of gin and a bottle of sherry!'

It soon became an evening routine to sit out on the stoep (veranda) after my bath and before 'chop' (dinner) while the steward boy, when called, served drinks from his tray – usually whisky. While the term whisky/soda was always bandied about, I, like most people preferred, and still do, whisky and water. In those days, however, there were one or two old Coasters who possessed 'soda streams'. These were large gas cylinders about five feet long and provided enough soda to last for weeks before recharging was needed. I am not sure where the recharging took place, but perhaps the Public Works Department would oblige. It was usually said that one should not drink whisky in the tropics before sundown, or at least not till the sun was well 'over the yardarm'. Hence the term 'sundowners'. However, this rule did not appear to apply to beer or gin!

As assistant to Scott, I was to help in the administration of

10

agriculture in the Central Province, which stretched from Cape Coast in the south and then some 70 or 80 miles to the Ashanti border on the Pra river. After Hughes had gone on leave I purchased, second-hand, an American Chevrolet car for £60, and which was essential for travelling in the district. Also another necessity: an Electrolux kerosene-fuelled refrigerator. It is now most surprising to recollect that I was obliged to get an overdraft of £15 from the bank to pay for it!

North of Assuansi cocoa was a popular crop, though its cultivation was confined to small peasant farmers. Cocoa is a crop that requires damp humid conditions to thrive, and it is usually planted under large forest trees to provide shade and a moist atmosphere. At that time conditions were becoming somewhat marginal for the crop in parts of the province with some reduction of the necessary overhead shade. One of my duties was to establish nurseries of suitable shade trees such as cassias, erythrinas and gliricidias for issuing to the farms and, to publicise this aim, meetings were held with farmers in their villages where I was often accompanied by the Assistant District Commissioner from Cape Coast. One's remarks in English were interpreted by an African junior officer. With hindsight, some of the dieback of cocoa experienced might later have been attributed to Swollen Shoot virus.

On the station itself, the day usually started with a walk round accompanied by one or more of the station overseers. It is interesting to recall that in those days the wearing of a sun helmet was considered essential out of doors between the hours of 8.00 a.m. and 4.00 p.m. Otherwise sunstroke was considered a distinct likelihood! When I first came out to the Coast, I was equipped with a khaki 'Wolseley' helmet for everyday use and a white Bombay bowler for best. Only latterly and during the war did such serious precautions appear to become unnecessary. Shorts, bush jackets and stockings were approved everyday wear. Spine pads on the bush jackets were also considered essential at the time, but later became more the subject for jokes at did the non-existent 'tsetse belts'! Our inspection during the morning walk included the station flock of sheep which, accompanied by their shepherd, grazed all day on a cover crop of centrosema. Mutton at six old pence a pound was a popular perk for the station Europeans.

I didn't seem to have a lot of time for my old hobby of ornithology. In the tropics birds tend to make their presence felt by their garish plumage or unusual calls. I must mention, however, the bulbuls that woke me every morning at dawn with their little ditty 'Bring tea quickly Kofi' and the plaintive hoo, hoo, hoo of the Senegal coucal. Attempts to examine nests in citrus trees often resulted in being attacked by swarms of vicious red ants. Lighting in the bungalow was by Tilley lamp, and in the rainy season particularly, we had to get used to a bombardment of flying ants, sausage flies, moths, etc.

A feature of the forest country, and particularly at Assuansi, was the nightly calling of tree bears. The series of weird calls started low, but then gradually rose in pitch and tempo, ending in a final crescendo. The tree bear should be more correctly called the tree hyrax, and most amazingly its nearest relative is said to be the elephant! Later on I was able to confirm that, while common in the forest country of the colony, it had not crossed the Volta river into Togoland. Mona monkeys with their characteristic guttural call of 'wa hu, wa hu' often played around high up in the trees near the bungalow.

The rainy season developed in June and July, and though all-day rainfall was uncommon, there were almost daily heavy downpours, mainly in the late afternoons. Humidity increased, and clothes left out at night could be saturated in the morning, and shoes became covered in mould if not cleaned daily. One night at the end of June, the Gold Coast experienced an appreciable earthquake, though it lasted only half a minute. I was at the time having drinks at Scott's bungalow when there was a tremendous subterranean rumbling, accompanied by violent shaking. Needless to say we were soon outside on the stoep. The possibility of a more severe aftershock made me somewhat nervous for a week or two, but luckily, what aftershocks that did develop were only mild ones. The main centre of the earthquake, however, was Accra, from where a number of fatalities were reported, and apparently nobody slept indoors for several nights.

Visits were made to Cape Coast once or twice a week for shopping and the collection of mail, and sometimes at night to play snooker at the club. Opportunities for entertaining at Assuansi were rather limited, but my cook soon showed himself an expert at producing four or five course dinners. However, his boast at being able to tie table napkins in a number of different ways could not be fully tested out. At dinner parties African cooks liked to include a savoury course on the menu, even if it was only cod roes on toast. Sad to say, savouries seem to have gone out of fashion in England nowadays, unless you patronise the Savoy or Scott's in the West End. There was always something of a ritual when the meal was announced – the ladies repaired to the indoor facilities while the men trooped into the garden 'to see Africa'.

In July tragedy struck, proving that the Gold Coast was indeed an integral part of the White Man's Grave. First of all Mrs Scott learnt that her daughter, aged two, had died in England. She returned home at once, and I drove to Takoradi with Scott to see her off on the mailboat. It was a great treat to have drinks and dinner on the ship again but worse was to come. Scott, who had complained for some time of stomach upsets, was taken ill while I was away on a trek* at a rest house some 60 miles away. On receiving a telegram – 'Scott admitted hospital in Takoradi, return at once' – I did indeed return at once, but unfortunately Scott died two days later at Takoradi hospital of a perforated ulcer. I again drove through with some of the more senior staff to attend the

*In West Africa, travelling overnight with rest house accommodation or when camping was always referred to as 'on trek'. In East Africa the corresponding term was 'on safari'

13

funeral. It seems inconceivable that such a tragedy could occur nowadays.

Another Agricultural Officer eventually arrived to take over Scott's place, an Irishman named Packham. Soon afterwards I received notification that I was shortly to transfer to Head Office in Accra as a temporary replacement for the departmental secretary.

Before transfer, here are a few more interesting features of life at Assuansi and on the Coast in general. Scott's cook was an enthusiastic hunter and he often brought us excellent 'bushmeat'. Going along forest paths at night with an acetylene lamp on his head and carrying his gun, he encountered bewildered duikers (small antelope). It was apparent that many villagers possessed old-fashioned firearms, usually referred to as Dane guns. These, presumably, were bartered by the early traders for local produce, perhaps even slaves. It is possible that the firing of such guns would in some cases bring more danger to the firer than to the quarry!

The habit of Africans carrying loads on their heads soon became a normal sight to me. Newly arrived visitors, however, might be rather astonished to see children going to school with their ink pots on their heads, or to be passed by a seamstress carrying on her head an undoubtedly heavy sewing machine. Another common head load was the ubiquitous four-gallon petrol or kerosene tin – the habitual container for water, palm oil, etc. Such methods produced attractive upright figures. Perhaps I should explain that the mammy or other carrier did not balance the load directly on to the head, but used a ring of cloth to form a more level carrying base.

As far as possible the village African tends to use local resources for everyday purposes. He never for instance requires string. The forest provides numerous lianas for use as 'tie tie'. If it rains, just cut a banana leaf. The African has excellent teeth, using freshly-cut chewing sticks every day instead of toothbrushes.

From the smallest village to the largest town, the centre of activity is always the market place. Apart from the one or more large weekly markets when the people flock in from far and wide, there is always some trade going on. On a full market day, apart from the fresh foodstuffs, there are innumerable other commodities on view, e.g. cotton goods, cheap tinned fish (tinappa), kitchen utensils, medicines both proprietary and native, palm wine, etc., etc.

4

Head Office Accra – August/September 1939

I moved to Accra on August 7th 1939, and took over the comparatively 'smallboy' post of secretary at Head Office. Without the district travel I found the work somewhat boring. However, there were distinct advantages in being in Accra with such mod cons as electric light, running water and radio rediffusion. Accra at that time had a population of some 1,000 Europeans, and there were of course many shops and stores, and a large European club which, believe it or not, had two billiard tables, one with an attendant marker!

My duties at Head Office were not particularly onerous, and largely centred around the offices of the seven or eight senior officers. It now seems strange to recall how in those days officers communicated with each other by messenger, sending backwards and forwards a series of numbered minutes. These could amount to as many as twenty or thirty before a 'discussion' could be concluded! Even at Assuansi with only two Europeans in adjoining offices the same procedure was maintained, rather than walk into the next office to discuss the matter verbally!

However, there was an additional duty for the secretary which brought some variety. I was also the officer in charge of the important-sounding Accra Horticultural and Arboricultural Society, which qualified me for an additional allowance of £6 a month. The society had nurseries in Accra raising ornamental trees and shrubs largely for the beautification of the residential areas. Hibiscus, bougainvillea, plumbago and pride of Barbados were among the most popular shrubs and were distributed free of charge. Partly for this reason, and because people took great pride in their gardens, the poor secretary often found himself at the mercy of some very formidable wives of very senior civil servants.

The climate of Accra was of a very reasonable nature, with the temperatures seldom exceeding the mid-eighties in the middle part of the day, and there was usually a nice breeze off the sea at this time. At night, however, the breeze dropped and conditions then tended to become a little sticky. While the bungalow was some one or two miles from the beach, one could always hear the roar of the heavy surf. Although the rainfall in Accra was not high, downpours could be heavy, hence the deep storm drains in the main streets of Accra and other larger towns.

It was in Accra that I first made the acquaintance of the itinerant Hausa man and learnt how to haggle. Such characters made the round of the European bungalows in particular, displaying a large range of ornamental commodities, some of undoubted African charm, others perhaps brassware from Birmingham and of little account. However, to a newcomer like me, a number of cheap and colourful articles could be bought to decorate an otherwise sparsely furnished bungalow. Wares on display would include attractive leather pouffes and cushions and Kano cloth from the Northern Territories, all sorts of brassware, Indian carpeting, crocodile and lizard skin handbags and, at that time, leopard skins and ivory ornaments. Later on at Kpeve I purchased and still possess a very well carved ebony and ivory chess set. Other attractive items for sale would include carved African heads, Ashanti stools and animal figures. The finest ivory carving I ever saw was a splendid hippopotamus which a Greek called Frankiglou had imported from French Country.

Before August was out, rumours of war became more frequent,

and when it did break out, I joined the Gold Coast Regiment which forms part of the Royal West African Frontier Force. As a result, on 20th September I was called up and ordered to join the second battalion of the regiment, then stationed at Tamale in the Northern Territories. Having put my heavy loads into storage, I travelled by car to Tamale, staying the night at Kumasi on the way with several other embryo officers and non-commissioned officers (NCOs).

Mamoba country

18

5

In the Army – September 1939 to May 1940

Tamale, the capital of the Northern Territories (the NTs), is some 240 miles from Kumasi where I had stayed the night. After leaving Kumasi, forest country prevailed until we had descended from the Mampong scarp, some 40 miles on the way. Then the vegetation changed to orchard bush, with the trees interspersed with tall elephant grass and this continued all the way. A well-known water supply officer of my acquaintance and rather appropriately named T. Hirst (i.e. Thirst!) always referred to this type of bush as good 'MAMOBA' country. When you asked what that was, he triumphantly replied, 'Miles and miles of bloody Africa'! The Ashanti border was reached at Yeji, where the Volta river is crossed by a large car ferry. This was not normally driven by mechanical means but swung with the current from one bank to the other using a series of buoys. Only when the river was low was the ferry motorised.

At Tamale I joined several other conscripts – those that were formerly in the local forces were officers, and others like myself and lacking this qualification were British non-commissioned officers, i.e. platoon sergeants. The government generously maintained the salaries of conscripted civil servants throughout the war. Indeed, one member of the legal department was rumoured to be the highest paid sergeant in the British army. Tamale was the headquarters of the 2nd battalion of the Gold Coast Regiment, and the plan was to bring this unit up to the strength of a full scale battalion for subsequent service overseas. There was of course already in residence a complement of regular European officers and NCOs. Tamale had the dubious reputation of experiencing in 1931 the last outbreak of yellow fever known in the colony. Several of the twenty or so European residents died.

Nearly all the infantry soldiers in the Gold Coast were from the Northern Territories or from the French colonies still further to the north. Different tribes were distinguished by their deeply cut facial markings. While they all spoke different tongues, they quickly picked up the language of the regiment, Hausa, and also a 'pidgin' English. Southerners usually did not make suitable fighting soldiers and if recruited were generally employed as clerks, cooks or drivers.

I was posted to B Company as Platoon Sergeant though I soon took over as Company Quartermaster Sergeant to relieve the regular occupant of this post who was going on leave. The work was mainly concerned with the provisioning, paying out and issuing clothes and equipment to the newly recruited soldiers. This, incidentally, avoided a certain proportion of the outdoor training work, which may have been thought to have some advantage in the very hot conditions then prevailing.

Tamale, in common with all parts of the NTs, is a very hot station with afternoon temperatures rising into the nineties, particularly in the period October to April. As far as possible, training was carried out in the early mornings, with rest in the afternoons and parades when required in the evenings.

At first I shared a bungalow with a regular NCO and meals were taken in the Sergeants' Mess. Food was reasonably good at that time and there was a well-stocked bar. The station had the usual European club where activity tended to concentrate round

Second Battalion, Tamale, 1940

the snooker table. Play was often interrupted by having to remove from the table large numbers of moths and sausage flies attracted by the lights. Both the regular NCOs and officers played polo. Polo here was reputed to be the cheapest in the world with the ponies, usually imported from the French country costing as little as £10 apiece. Shooting was also popular and mainly concerned guinea fowl and francolin (a type of partridge).

Full scale parades of the battalion were regularly held and Colonel Hayes, the Commanding Officer, frequently gave pep talks to the African troops advising how they should deal with the 'King's enemies.' I also well remember a discourse by Major Reade, the Adjutant, seriously reminding us more-recently recruited Europeans: 'You may wear Australian hats, but we will not accept Australian discipline!' He referred of course to our slouch hats and perhaps our rather irresponsible attitude.

On October 18th I travelled to Accra, still in my faithful car, to attend a four-week course of instruction at what was soon to be

21

referred to as the 'School of Destruction'. This was held at canton-
ments some two miles from the centre of the town. This course
proved to us previously sheltered individuals to be a somewhat
harrowing experience. The day started with PT and then all sorts
of lectures and exercises, not to mention route marches.
Manoeuvres were carried out on the neighbouring Accra plains
including a particularly exhausting night operation. I well
remember when we returned from this rather late at night, we
found, perhaps not surprisingly, that the bar was closed! I believe
I was marched with others before the CO next morning accused
of breaking into it!

Food at the School of Destruction was at first terrible. It was
indeed organised by the Syrian who provided me a few months
earlier with my up-country supplies. I would, however, have
credited him with sufficient experience not to serve beetroot and
cream as a sweet! However, things did improve, and I still
maintained the car to go into town in the evenings, either to the
club or the one and only hotel at that time – the Seaview.

After four weeks, back again to Tamale where there were now
certain alterations. We were billeted in round huts with thatched
roofs at a local school just outside Tamale, and there had been
some deterioration in the food. We had also had an influx of white
Rhodesians, both officers and NCOs, who had been recruited to
make up the full establishment of the battalion. They soon inte-
grated with us Britishers and we got on well together for the rest
of the war. I would also like to say that in due course they came to
have a high regard for the Gold Coast troops.

I would like to make it clear here that, when I rather pointedly
differentiate between Europeans and Africans, this is not done
with any sense of racialism. At that time there were only a handful
of Africans appointed as senior officers in government service,
and in the army none at all. It was, however, the policy of the
colonial government to prepare the Africans for eventual self-
government. Although it may be argued that progress in this aim

was somewhat slow at that time, I am sure that this policy, together with the fair and friendly way in which we treated the African, assisted in avoiding the unpleasant happenings that occurred in the Belgian Congo and in the ex Italian and Portuguese colonies at a later date.

We spent Christmas at Tamale with the usual celebrations. Soon after that, large scale manoeuvres lasting several days were carried out in the bush. As conditions were prevailingly dry at that time of year our camp beds were erected under the stars. This was the time of the year that the northern part of the colony especially comes under the influence of the harmattan, a drying wind blowing from the Sahara. This brings very hot and dusty conditions during the day, but with appreciable drops in temperature at night when even a blanket can be appreciated!

While travelling the roads through the bush at night, I first spotted the standard winged nightjar. The male of this species presents an extraordinary sight on the wing, as its long plumes furnished with broad webs on their ends float out behind the bird, giving the impression in the gloaming that two small bats are chasing it. All over Africa other nightjars arise mysteriously from the road in front of the car as the lights disturb them.

When working away from headquarters all camping gear, provisions and general stores had to be carried as head loads by the carriers and porters who formed a section of all West African regiments. Needless to say, head loads of Accra beer were included, and as these were crates of 48 bottles of one and a half pint capacity, it represented quite a weight for the poor carriers to struggle with! Unfortunately, for us if not for them, we could hardly transport refrigerators as well, so such beer was always tepid. Back at Tamale we changed our round houses for grass huts prepared by the troops, and at that time it was not necessary for them to be rainproof.

The time was now approaching for us to leave for the coast, in readiness for any possible overseas move. My company was selected as an advance party, and we camped for the first night at Yeji, though in actual fact we were there for a fortnight, as an outbreak of cerebral meningitis in the north held up the movement of the rest of the battalion, and we were isolated.

This, however, proved to be a very pleasant interlude. All senior officers and BNCOs camped out in the large thatched government rest house, enjoying the close proximity of the river Volta, which must have been about a quarter of a mile wide at this point. Hippos and crocodiles were said to be in the vicinity but we never saw any, despite several boat trips and our bathing in the river. Large herds of cattle destined for Accra and the coast, and under the supervision of several drovers, passed through Yeji while we were there. They did not use the ferry but were obliged to swim across the river.

Such cattle had to walk some 400 to 500 miles from the French country in the north to the coast. Animals that fell by the wayside were readily saleable in local villages en route, however emaciated. As Company Quartermaster Sergeant I was able to vary the company's diet with fish from the river and bushmeat (antelope or duiker), while rice and yams could be bought with ease. The local police sergeant volunteered to guide me to shoot a bush cow (African buffalo) but I thought that this might have been a little too dangerous and declined! There were large game fish in the river, notably Volta salmon and tiger fish. We did not, of course, throw in gelignite as we saw later in East Africa, resulting in many dead or stunned fish rising to the surface. An even worse ploy was to pour DDT into the river.

It was February before the battalion finally reached the coast and we made camp near the sea at Weija, some six miles from Accra, and where we Europeans were accommodated two at a time in fairly commodious tents. My days alternated with quarter-master work and as Acting Platoon Commander, also training and exercises on the surrounding plains. A more important affair altogether was brigade manoeuvres. While the 1st battalion was

24

camped close by, the 3rd battalion were enforced to march from Winneba some 60 miles away to take part.

We had a very wet period in March when the camp became a morass and we were almost cut off from Accra. We were fairly well off in our tents, but our mess and the grass and bamboo structures erected for our cooks collapsed. Conditions further deteriorated in May with the advent of the main rainy season, and there were scares with sightings of snakes and scorpions among the tents. As evidence of the high humidity that pertains on the coast, after sitting out one night on the beach, a box of gramophone needles left open were rusted completely by the morning.

Turning again to the quartermaster work; rations including both fresh fish and meat were reasonably available. Chickens had a great advantage for exercises away from camp – they could be carried alive! At that time of the year the afternoon sea breeze seemed to blow particularly strongly, which was annoying when sorting papers in the open tent. It was interesting to read in an old letter of mine that I was required to work late on the accounts because of the end of the financial year. While this may sound rather familiar nowadays, it seems a bit odd 50 years ago, with a war on, to talk about the financial year!

I was still maintaining my car which allowed visits to the club, etc. in Accra. I also attended several days of an Accra race meeting which supported a tote but no bookmakers. Syrians raced most of the horses and they no doubt were responsible for the greater part of the betting. In May it was rumoured that we should be soon leaving for an 'unknown' destination, and activities within the camp increased perceptibly with the constant blowing of bugle calls summoning CSMs, CQMSs, etc. I was responsible for issuing boots to all African staff in the company, not an easy task as they had never worn footwear before and had very broad feet. I sold the car to a Syrian for £25, which at that time seemed a perfectly reasonable price.

6

The Voyage to East Africa – June 1940

The 12th African Division of the West African Frontier Force sailed for East Africa early in June 1940. At Takoradi we embarked on an ex-cruise liner, the *Reino del Pacifico*, owned by the Canadian Pacific Line. The ship had been modified for trooping only as far as the provision of the men's mess decks and sleeping accommodation was concerned, and the ship still maintained its passenger lounges and many first class cabins. I as an NCO was privileged to have a cabin to myself with a bed, not a bunk! Meals were excellent, as were the bars which of course were very well patronised.

Few of our African troops had ever seen the sea. As soon as we left Takoradi harbour behind we encountered, perhaps unusually, a rather choppy motion. This caused some initial disorganisation and sea sickness on the mess decks. Things improved, however, and the men got used to their unusual surroundings and settled down well. On one particular calm day out from Takoradi we saw the unusual sight of a number of individual whales spouting. The ship's crew later agreed that our African troops were generally better behaved and cleaner than the European troops they had previously carried.

The convoy, escorted by a Royal Navy cruiser, included several other liners carrying the battalions of the Nigerian Regiment.

Every morning our troops stood to at 6.15 a.m. for PT. The days were occupied with lectures, boat drills, etc. There was of course plenty of activity in the bars when off duty, as far as the Europeans were concerned. I remember taking part in various gambling games including the notorious Crown and Anchor with somewhat mixed results.

As we progressed towards the Cape, the weather turned colder and the seas rougher. The troops certainly did not appreciate the former, and there was at least one death through pneumonia. It was planned that we should dock at Capetown, but very heavy seas made this impracticable, and we had perforce to steam on to Simonstown where we anchored offshore, but again without shore leave.

Then on to Durban where we disembarked and stayed for four days. We Europeans were accommodated in railway carriages, and the troops nearby in large railway sheds. We were royally welcomed by the residents who entertained us out to meals, dances, etc. and provided lifts all over the place. It is rather sad to relate that our own soldiers did not have a similar reception, and because of apartheid regulations they were not legally allowed to purchase beer or alcoholic beverages. The battalion conducted a route march through some of the residential areas of Durban to show the flag, and the troops were much impressed by the many multi-storey buildings and the large number of white people. The latter were, however, more than a little surprised when our troops fell out for their usual hourly break during the march. They, the troops, had not realised that they should not openly relieve themselves on the side of the road as they would have done on the Coast.

At Durban we transferred to a much smaller ship, the *Ranchi* of the British India Line. Still a bar, but shared cabins, and a lot of curries on the menu which was of course no bad thing. We sailed unescorted for nearly a fortnight up the East African coast, through the Mozambique channel between Africa and Madagascar, and arrived eventually at Mombasa, the main port of Kenya.

27

7

Kenya. To the Northern Frontier District

On disembarking at Mombasa we lost no time in boarding the train to take us up-country. Leaving at night time, we were woken at daylight by excited shouts of 'Nyama Nyama' (bushmeat) from the African soldiers. We were clearly travelling through the Tsavo game reserve and the troops were astonished by the abundant animal life, seemingly oblivious of the train. In their sub-Saharan hinterlands large game animals were few and far between, though viewed with great interest as possible additions to their diet. There were numerous antelopes, wildebeest, zebra, giraffe and ostriches all grazing contentedly. The countryside seemed sparsely populated, though there were always Africans to meet the train when it stopped at the small and occasional stations. These stations seemed to be in charge of Indian station-masters who supervised loading the firewood which fed the engines.

We saw no more of Nairobi than we did of Mombasa, but travelled on about a further 100 miles to Nanyuki, which was the end of the line. Nanyuki was a township some 6,000 feet in altitude and the centre for many European farms. Most of the shops were dukas (Indian-run stores) which typically sold a wide range of goods both for the African and European populations. We were housed in log cabins in the forest, and because of the altitude, conditions were very cold at night, particularly when taking an outside camp bath in the evenings. At all times the snowy peaks of Mount Kenya were in sight.

We spent a lot of our spare time in the Silverbeck Hotel which I believe was very well-known locally, though the officer classes patronised a rival hotel, the Sportsman's Arms. I was rather impressed, when visiting a café which the locals had opened to entertain the troops, to be told by a lady helper that on the way to work that morning their transport had been held up by elephants on the road.

At that time the Italians had not long entered the war – actually on 10 June 1940 – and their troops had adopted threatening positions all along the wild Abyssinian and Somali borders with Kenya. The British outpost at Moyale had already been evacuated and indeed the defending forces in Kenya were heavily out-numbered. At first the defence of the colony had been solely in the hands of only six battalions of the locally recruited King's African Rifles, the KAR. The arrival of our two West African brigades however helped to maintain the balance. To add to the racial mix, we also encountered at Nanyuki a detachment of an Indian field battery, and several times later small sections of the Somaliland Camel Corps.

At the time of our arrival, the Italian armed forces in Abyssinia were said to number some 200,000 men who were supported by many planes. While at that time it did seem conceivable that such large forces would be capable of advancing into the heart of Kenya and causing mayhem, in retrospect that would have seemed to be unlikely. Their colonial troops of Italian origin were not thought to be of very high calibre, which was to reflect on the discipline and expertise of their native soldiers which, like our own, formed the larger proportion of the two opposing armies. In the coming battles their Eritrean soldiers gained the reputation of being the Italians' most reliable conscripts. One must also mention the Banda. These were bands of guerilla soldiers, usually commanded by one or more Europeans, and who had a roving capacity.

The Banda were, generally speaking, an ill-disciplined bunch, mostly Somalis with no recognised uniforms and little or no experience of any military training. They were paid, but did not draw rations and so were expected to live on the country. Thus they were not very popular among the more peaceful tribes of the frontier. They were tough and cruel and had a primitive lust for fighting, providing perhaps it was not against well-armed opposition.

One must not confuse the Banda with the Shifta. The Shifta were groups of Abyssinian irregulars, patriots who also roamed the wild borders, though on our side. Their leaders were mostly Kenya Europeans and particularly from the White Hunter fraternity. One of their principals was Jack Bonham, an ex-game warden, whom we encountered later at Marsabit. He claimed that, by the end of 1940, there were as many as 60,000 Shifta in southern Abyssinia.

It was clear that even if the Italians had 200,000 troops at their disposal, their logistical problems were many and varied. Apart from the fact that they were holding down a huge territory which contained many different peoples generally unfriendly to them, their borders were equally immense. Apart from our Kenya borders, those with the Sudan stretched for hundreds of miles, while the countries of Eritrea and Somaliland, not long annexed, risked invasion from the Red Sea. The only saving grace for the Italians was, perhaps, that their Eritrean and Somali subjects did not like the Abyssinians any more than they did the Italians. This perhaps explains how the Italians were able to recruit good fighting material from these two conquered territories.

After a week at Nanyuki my company, 'B', was detached from the battalion and ordered to travel to Marsabit, an outpost not far from the Abyssinian border, and there to take over from a company of the KAR. Travelling by lorry, we descended from the high ground and on to the plain, which led in due course to the Northern Frontier Province. The advantages for travelling by road transport soon became obvious as we passed on our way companies of our 1st battalion who had been instructed to march to Isiolo, a three days' journey. They were finding the going exceedingly arduous and, believe it or not, there were many stragglers. Excuses can be made: the men had taken very little exercise during the past six weeks and the long voyage from West Africa had hardly been a toughening experience. Moreover, the road wound steeply down from the escarpment from a height of 6,000 feet to the grilling heat and the dusty red boulders of the plain. However, I am sure that this temporary dent in the regiment's reputation was fully retrieved later on. We passed an unforgettable sight, a white farmer with a waggon drawn by at least a dozen oxen, a method of transport even unusual at the time we were there, and now a thing of the past.

We crossed into the fabulous Northern Frontier District at Archers Post on the Uaso Nyiro river. The NFD is an immense desert area some 100,000 square miles in extent, which represents almost half of Kenya. It is almost entirely thornbush and sand with infrequent water-holes, sometimes 50 miles apart, and the rainfall would seldom exceed ten inches a year. This country is so arid and sparsely populated, and at times raided by hostile tribes from over the Abyssinian border, as to be entered in peacetime only by permit and with a police or military escort. Nevertheless, the country has a great deal of fascination, particularly as much game is present.

We took two days to reach Marsabit over atrocious roads, and when camping for the night, we were warned to keep a look-out for elephants and lions! We frequently crossed wadis where we descended into dried-up river beds where there were occasional groves of dom palms and acacia trees. Not much game was in evidence, though at some of the river beds abundant droppings and tracks were to be seen. For many miles of our journey the forbidding-looking Mathews Range accompanied us on our left side. Eventually Marsabit Mountain came into view, and we started

31

to ascend through a gradual transition from the thornbush to orchard bush, and eventually almost rainforest conditions at a height of 4,000 to 5,000 feet.

Wajir Fort

8

Marsabit – 1940

Marsabit is such a unique geographical feature in Kenya that I consider it merits a chapter to itself. It is a mountain some 5,000 feet in height and has an area of some 800 square miles. It is completely isolated by miles and miles of sandy wastes and thornbush country, and lies almost equidistant between the commencement of the NFD at Archers Post and Isiolo and the Abyssinian border. Marsabit Mountain has a climate of its own. Moist winds all the way from the Indian Ocean collide with the high ground on the mountain, and there condense to cloud and fog, thus encouraging tropical rainforest. Trees are covered with skeins of moss and lichens and there are several volcanic lakes.

After taking over from the company of KARs we camped in the forest not far from the District Officer's headquarters, the Boma, as it was always referred to in East Africa. Our retainers put up grass huts for our camp beds and we took over the mess recently vacated by our predecessors. Surrounded as we were by forest, the nights especially rang with animal cries that at times amounted to what seemed violent disturbances. These were mainly attributable to elephants and baboons possibly disturbed by leopards. Hyenas were always 'laughing' close by and actually started entering our tents at night, even removing boots and articles of clothing. When, however, the 'wolves', as the soldiers called

33

them, started to take away large tins of meat, some element of doubt arose. It was thought possible that human wolves might have been involved!

After the traditional army 'stand to' before dawn, my platoon spent most of the day fortifying a point on the main approach road, which we came to refer to as the SOB, otherwise 'shit or bust' corner. We were given here the classical ultimatum that this position was to be defended to the 'last man and the last round'! While we were carrying on the digging of a series of trenches, we were observed with great interest by a large family of baboons. The old males were very formidable creatures, and it was amusing to see the females carrying their young about on their backs. A common feature of the landscape here was large cacti some ten to twelve feet high (Euphorbia Candelabra). From our altitude on the mountain, we could see over miles and miles of the surrounding desert. 'Dust devils' crossing the plain were often in evidence, and at times we wondered whether or not they could be

Approaching Mount Marsabit

34

approaching Italian convoys. This was the Chalbi Desert, which was said to flood not infrequently after heavy rains. I would always have liked to visit the fabulous Lake Rudolph which lay away to the west.

The forest was interspersed on the summit and on the lower slopes with patches of more open grassland where game was plentiful. We often saw the rare greater kudu, a large antelope with very long horns. Here I saw my first gerenuk, perhaps the strangest buck in Africa. They possessed long giraffe-like necks, and by standing on their hind legs were able to reach the leaves of thornbush trees as much as ten feet from the ground. Oryx were also common, as were the ubiquitous tail-wagging Thompson gazelles and the leaping impalas. Large bustards were much in evidence, though my attempts to shoot one with a 303 rifle were, not surprisingly, unsuccessful!

My platoon took it in turns to spend a few days at a time guarding a small airfield, sleeping at night in underground dugouts. No air raids took place while we were there, though Italian Capronis and Savoias had made aggressive visits on previous occasions. Several visits were made to the airstrip by our own pilots in Hawker Hart bi-planes. Platoon commanders increased their popularity with their men by shooting game as extra rations. I was not too popular – only one zebra! While there seemed to be a complete absence of mosquitos, tsetses and biting flies on Marsabit, we were much troubled by ticks, which attached themselves unbeknown, particularly under the tops of puttees and often higher up! Near our airstrip was a gravestone of a European who had been killed by an elephant. I only saw elephant once, a small group near the road. They were red, through wallowing in muddy waters, and quickly disappeared when they spotted us. While in camp I sometimes took solitary walks, somewhat warily however. My 4.5 revolver might not have been a suitable weapon to face a hostile buffalo!

In the more open areas great displays of gay wild flowers

abounded, and everywhere were brilliantly plumaged birds – rollers, sun birds, and bee eaters. Colobus monkeys were common in the trees surrounding the camp. The local inhabitants were predominately of the Boran tribe and there were also itinerant Somalis. Some natives lived locally with their cattle, sheep and goats, while others visited the mountain less frequently to water their camels. One often met men in odd places walking along laden only with a spear. A few yards behind would be the wife, bowed down with a load of personal belongings on her back.

The largest lake on the mountain is Lake Paradise, where the film 'Congorilla' was made some time before the war. The Company Commander thought he would give us a break one Sunday morning so that we might visit the lake. It required quite a walk to reach it, ascending as we did steep forest paths clearly regularly used by elephants. Their huge footprints were much in evidence all round the lake, and some of our troops were eager to fill any convenient tins with their dung which was said to be a strong juju in their own country. There must have been a great congregation of game drinking at night, though when we were there in the day, local tribesmen were watering their cattle with a few camels and donkeys. The cattle on the mountain always looked incredibly sleek, despite the dry-looking grasses. These were, as in other parts of Africa, kept as cash in the bank and used almost solely for milk production, though the owners also drew off blood from the neck to drink, as the Masai did. Our soldiers, however, were sometimes able to purchase a local fat-tailed sheep for a celebratory meal.

Many water birds were present on the lake including spoonbills, marabout storks, hammercops and many smaller species. There were large flocks of African coots, but I was only to discover later that surprisingly there were no fish in the lake, though there were plenty of large frogs which provided ample food for a resident pair of fish eagles.

While there was plenty of water in the lake when we were

there, I am told that it can get low in times of drought. Later in the war, and before the invasion of Abyssinia commenced, two South African Brigade groups were based at Marsabit for a time, and then water actually had to be brought in by truck.

My company spent about two months at Marsabit, leaving only once to send a motorised patrol towards the Abyssinian frontier. After descending from the mountain we emerged on the Didi Galla plain which lies to the north and east of the mountain. This country must resemble parts of the moon. The surface for miles is completely covered by small black volcanic boulders, over which it is impossible to drive and very tiring to walk over. However, we encountered an exceedingly rough road that had been constructed through this terrain and led towards the frontier, some 100 miles distant. Our objective was a small border post known as Sololo, where we were expected to bump the enemy. We travelled in a convoy of trucks, and of course were accompanied by a small section of Abyssinian irregulars for security purposes. Some twenty miles short of the frontier, however, the road cuts through a low range known as the Turbi Hills. We debussed while the leading platoon entered the pass through the hills, only to come under fire from a detachment of Banda who were in occupation. After a limited skirmish and with night not far away, it was decided to withdraw, walking for the first mile or two in case we were enfiladed from the flanks.

I have frequently thought, in retrospect, that if the Italians had held their fire until the company, or part of it, had negotiated the pass and reached the other side, we would have found ourselves in a very difficult position. The terrain was so rough that there would have been no way back for vehicles except on the one narrow road.

After our interesting months at Marsabit, the company transferred to Wajir, another important placename in the Northern Frontier District.

9

Wartime in the NFD.
Wajir, 1940–41

The outpost of Wajir was some hundred miles east of Marsabit. In peacetime it represented the northern headquarters of the King's African Rifles, and a convenient centre for the supervision of the long and wild frontiers of Abyssinia and Italian Somaliland where so many belligerent tribes held sway.

The fort at Wajir was reminiscent of Beau Geste with its white crenellated walls. Partly surrounding the fort was a town consisting of little more than a few shops and Indian dukas, a mosque and various residences. The thick walls of the fort kept conditions reasonably cool for its military residents, while reliable water holes made Wajir an important centre for camel routes leading towards and from the frontier. While Wajir Fort was a hot, dusty, fly-ridden centre by day, it has been described as particularly beautiful by moonlight!

There are reputed to be upwards of seventy reliable wells around Wajir, and there is always a big concentration of camels both coming and going. There may be several hundred present on any one day, and they may have to wait a day or two to be watered. The wells are deep and the water had to be drawn up by hand in goatskin buckets. Despite this the camels are well-disciplined and wait their turn patiently, through they do keep up an unending thirsty lament. After watering, the camels are driven back into the bush, and it may be a fortnight before they return again for their next drink.

We were camped in the thornbush outside the fort where we found the conditions very hot, dusty and arid. Talking about the water holes again, like most other sources of water in the NFD their taste was, to say the least, very brackish. For us Europeans the only way to make this water palatable was to add lime juice. People who drank too much of these waters tended to suffer from a malady vulgarly referred to as 'Wajir Clap'.

We of course continued to carry out our exercises and patrols. One of my platoon's tasks was to spend three nights a week at a forward post some ten miles out of Wajir, and on the road to El Wak and the Abyssinian frontier. This camp was known as the Ruksa Post and was protected by Dainit wire. It was here that we heard for the first time lion roaring in the vicinity. There were usually giraffe in the surrounding bush and groups of oryx were common. We saw a number of dik-dik, very small antelopes little bigger than hares. They were reputed to require no water at all, living on the dew. Particularly on moonlit nights, blacksmith plovers somewhere in the vicinity seemed to live in a permanently disturbed state, keeping up a non-stop peevish outcry.

Nothing very exciting occurred at the Ruksa Post while we were in occupation, though East African armoured cars passed by on their patrols towards the frontier. These cars, having been locally constructed, appeared to us very vulnerable objects, being small civilian pick-up trucks with a driver in the front and another soldier in the back armed with a Bren gun. With no armour plating protection they seemed very exposed to ambush, and would not have stood up to the impact of land mines. Luckily the use of land mines did not figure commonly in the conduct of the East African campaign. After the war with Italy had been concluded, we learnt that our outpost had been observed, unbeknown to us, by a Banda patrol led by an Italian known as 'Twinkle Toes'. Presumably he had very small feet and was well known for his daring raids over this barren territory.

Conditions at Wajir and its neighbourhood were very hot and dry, with the temperatures probably rising into the high nineties in the afternoons. While we were camped at the Ruksa Post there were one or two unseasonable rainstorms, to our surprise causing the desert to bloom. In no time, grass and attractive flowers sprang up through the sand, and what had been bare shrubs bloomed.

During our stay at Wajir, we were pleased to receive a visit from the South African leader – General Smuts himself. His civilian plane was accompanied by two unfamiliar escorts. They were in fact Spitfires, the first that we had seen, and it was a measure of Smuts's importance that allowed their detachment from other main theatres of war. Up to now we had only seen more old-fashioned planes – Hawker Harts, Fairey Battles and Gloucester Gladiator bi-planes. While we were camped at Archers Post on another occasion we saw two of our Gladiators take on three Italian Caproni bombers, and although no planes were shot down, the Iti quickly left the scene, releasing their bombs well away from our positions.

By this time the East African Force had been reinforced by two South African divisions, with some of their battalions rather curiously named – the Natal Carbineers, the Transvaal Scottish and the Capetown Irish. With them of course were the usual complementary engineers and transport personnel. During the early part of the war, the main object in defending Kenya was to safe-guard the port of Mombasa, an important link in the line of com-munications between South Africa and the Middle East. It was certainly not the intention of the South African government to operate outside this theatre of war.

By late 1940 our fighting forces in Kenya had reached a total of 20,000 men. This force comprised some 22 battalions – nine South African, six East African, six West African and one Northern Rhodesian. History has recorded an argument that developed between Churchill and General Wavell. The former thought that the West and South African troops ought to be transferred to the Middle East, leaving the defence of the colony to East African resources alone. This I am sure would have left Kenya dangerously under-defended, particularly as Italian submarine activity based on the ports that they had occupied on the Horn of Africa was increasing. Luckily, General Wavell's plan to invade Abyssinia and defeat the Italians gained the day. This, if carried out successfully, would remove the threat to the rear of the Eighth Army in Egypt and Libya. It is also clear that the South Africans would not have agreed to the transfer of any of their forces to the Middle East.

The South African troops were destined to take part in the first major action of the war when, with part of the Gold Coast Brigade, they liberated El Wak, a strategic Italian outpost on the Somali border and very strongly defended. While it is true the enemy were heavily outnumbered, they had to retreat in some disorder and with many casualties and much lost equipment. Our losses were only two South Africans killed. After this the Italians' chances of striking had gone, and they withdrew in some disorder behind the line of the Juba river. Some time after this the Emperor Haile Selassie re-entered his country from the north. He raised his flag at Debra Markos and eventually triumphantly reached Addis Ababa on 5 May 1941.

Early in November 1940 I was given permission to take ten days' leave in Nairobi. I set off in a South African convoy of trucks but, as an example of the difficulties of the terrain, we were held up for five days at Habaswein in the Lorian Swamp, due to impassable rained-out roads. Imagine the boredom of five days camped in the thornbush with nothing to do! Things were not improved by an insect or its larvae which descended from the trees causing a lot of irritation. The symptoms had indeed earned the name of the Habaswein itch. I believe the Lorian Swamp becomes a swamp only in the wet season, though Habaswein lies in a drier part of it. In fact Habaswein in Swahili meant the 'Big

Dust'. Habaswein has always been associated with elephants, and somewhere within its boundaries is said to be a fabulous elephants' graveyard holding large stocks of ivory still to be located.

After Habaswein we spent a very different two nights at Nanyuki which was now full of very lively South African soldiers. The hotel rang to the strains of their favourite song which was all about a girl called Solly Marais down in the mealie fields. This refrain seemed to be the equivalent of what 'Waltzing Matilda' was to the Australians. Then by rail to Nairobi, passing many coffee and sisal plantations on the way. I always remembered that not only all the passenger compartments were fitted with bottle openers but the toilets as well! – a useless piece of information, I am afraid.

In Nairobi I stayed at the New Stanley Hotel. What a contrast to the NFD! I found later that in a letter home I had compared my room to one in the Regent Palace Hotel in London! I will, however, give a fuller description of Nairobi in the next chapter. It was rumoured during the course of my leave that I was to be transferred to headquarter work at Second Echelon in Nairobi. I received this news with very mixed feelings. While there were distinct advantages for living among the fleshpots, there were distinct drawbacks on the grounds of expense, and also there would be a guilty feeling of leaving my friends in the front line.

However, as there was no confirmation of this posting available in Nairobi, I made the long trip back to Wajir, only to be told on arrival to return straight back to Nairobi! And so I did. I will explain that in the army one makes journeys of this nature by availing oneself of any supply convoy that might be taking the desired road. The trucks in such convoys were usually South African manned, and any extra traveller would invariably be invited to share messing facilities with the drivers. One slept on the ground or possibly in the cab of a vehicle. On a peg to the right of the windscreen on every truck in East Africa rode a canvas water bag, kept cool by the breeze on its wet surface.

10

A Stay in Nairobi

The period in which I was attached to the West African Second Echelon in Nairobi was a time of boring office hours and considerable partying at other times. The Second Echelon is an organisation that in war time preserves the records of forward units in a place of comparative safety. It was not that the work was particularly uninteresting, but I believe we were overstaffed and there was not enough to do. I stayed at first in the well-known New Stanley Hotel, then in the Avenue Hotel, but later moved to a small hotel in the suburbs which cost as little as £7-10-0s a week, and that for full board! As, however, I invariably had lunch in town and went there again nearly every evening to consort with other contemporaries on leave, I hardly took full advantage of these generous terms.

Even as long ago as 1940, Nairobi was a fine city, and being at an altitude of some 6,000 feet, it had a very pleasant climate. Apart from the two major hotels in which I stayed, there were several other well-known ones including Torrs, the Queens and the Norfolk, famous for its associations with the early settler days. There were several cinemas, many shops and restaurants, a racecourse and other small hotels on the outskirts. Meals in the main hotels were very cheap and good, costing 3/- for lunch and 4/6 for dinner, both of several courses.

During my stay in Nairobi, great interest was being shown in the Lord Erroll/Sir Delves Broughton murder case. These unusual events largely concerned the white members of the so called 'Happy Valley' set, and whose activities were centred on the posh Muthaiga Country Club. Not a venue, incidentally, where a common platoon sergeant would be welcome! While this tragedy and its aftermath had no bearing on the course of the war, greater coverage of these bizarre events occurred in the well-produced East African Standard than of the course of the war itself. A full account of these happenings may be found in the book by James Fox, *White Mischief.* I would like to say, however, that while a proportion of the inhabitants of the so-called White Highlands did give Kenya a bad name in those days, they were a minority group, and there were many European settlers who carved their farms out of the bush with great diligence and hardship, and often with limited capital resources.

As I have already mentioned, we town 'residents' were continually meeting up with acquaintances coming on leave from their battalions up-country. As these individuals were very thirsty and wished to be shown the town, it was a tiring time! Among the visitors were two very attractive wives who had followed their non-commissioned husbands out from England – namely Dorothy Skidmore, whose husband was an agricultural officer, and Lela Roemelle, the wife of a DC. For some unknown reason the former had with her a Rhodesian Ridgeback dog which she asked me to keep in my room in the New Stanley Hotel overnight. Unfortunately, it did not behave itself very well and this led me to receive a very frosty reception from the management next day.

Eric Lanning, formerly in the 3rd battalion GCR, has provided me with the following information on Hugh and Lela Roemelle. 'Hugh joined 3GCR at Winneba with me. After we both got early UK leave we returned (June 1940) on the *Narkunda*, heading for Mombasa. Skidmore was also with us. On board was the delectable Lela (Austrian) bound for Singapore. She "jumped" ship at

Mombasa and came on to Nairobi with us where she and Hugh were married in the DC's office, Nairobi, late in July 1940. I was "best man". Lela was one helluva girl and they separated soon enough.' I understand from Eric Lanning that Lela died in Vienna some five or ten years ago, married at that time to the Finance Minister!

During my sojourn in Nairobi, the grand attack on Italian East Africa commenced. The invasion in the south was by Nigerians of the 12th African Division who proceeded up the coast through Kismayo and Brava to Mogadishu, while my own battalion attacked further north from Garissa to Liboi, Hargeissa, Afmadu and Bardera. Before crossing the Juba river, the battalion had to fight a very lively action at Bulo Erillo where we lost, several European officers and NCOs. There by the grace of God might I have been!

Meanwhile, in Nairobi I had made several requests to the authorities for permission to rejoin the battalion. This devotion to duty may seem a little bold, and there were indeed occasions later, particularly under fire, when I did rather regret my temerity! My steward boy Maxwell also seemed to have some reservations about staying in Nairobi, but perhaps for a different reason. He complained to me, 'Massa, this town he chop all my money'. I should perhaps explain here that in West African pidgin, food, particularly among Europeans, is referred to as 'chop', though in this case 'chop' is used as a verb indicating that his money was being eaten up.

Readers may think it a little strange that both NCOs and officers took their steward boys with them to the war in East Africa. Indeed the officers also had their orderlies. I must make it clear however 'boys' did not accompany their masters into forward fighting areas or on patrol.

45

11

Italian Somaliland. April 1941

At the very end of March my sedentary duties in Nairobi ended, and I thankfully joined a road convoy leaving for Italian Somaliland. As is usual at these times, I occupied a seat by the driver in one of the lorries, camping for the night when and where required. On the first night we reached Thika which is still in the European farming belt, and reminiscent of Elspeth Huxley and her book *The Flame Trees of Thika*. We of course spent the evening at the Blue Posts Hotel.

The next day we descended on to the plain and spent the night camped close to the Tana river at Garissa. Thick scrub clothed the banks, which at one time had the reputation of an abundant elephant population equipped with some of the largest ivory in Africa. No elephants were seen on this occasion, however. We bathed from the pontoon bridge over the river, though there must have been some risk of infection with bilharzia.

We crossed the Kenya frontier at Liboi with its particularly saline water holes, and then through Haweina and Afmadu to the coast port of Kismayu. Many signs of the war were apparent, including damaged and abandoned lorries and a number of wrecked planes on an airfield at Afmadu. This journey took several days and we passed through some particularly desolate country, partly thornbush and partly featureless desert. Game seemed

46

Mogadishu – Palarro del Governo

scarce, but from time to time we passed a few wandering tribesmen
with their cattle and camels. Mirages appeared on the horizon as
we drove along, but these apparently palm surrounded oases of
course never materialised.

We spent a night outside Kismayu, and next day went into town
where we bathed in the sea. There was a very nice sandy beach
more reminiscent of Bournemouth than the heavy surf of West
Africa. Kismayu itself was an old-fashioned port of the Arab type
with mosques, and dhows in the harbour. From Kismayu we
travelled up the coast road through such centres as Jelib, Brava
and Merka before finally reaching Mogadishu, the capital of Italian
Somaliland. On the way we passed several Italian farming districts
with white farm houses and plantations of bananas, coconuts and
cotton.

We found Mogadishu to be a comparatively modern and up-to-
date city with white buildings and palm lined streets and avenues,
and there were many Italians in evidence, including women and

children. The shops were very empty of goods, but restaurants had quite reasonable food. Pasta, beans, milk and eggs seemed to be in good supply, though there was a shortage of imported commodities. Bars were open but sold a pretty strange assortment of drinks. No beer or whisky, but such things as peppermint, vermouth, absinth and aniseed were available, together with some clearly locally prepared spirituous drinks of rather dubious origin which would perhaps have been better left alone!

An unpleasant feature of Mogadishu at that time, and for that matter to be found in most other Italian territories, was the terrible incidence of house flies. I recollect that if one was eating a piece of bread and jam one had to keep waving it in the air, or otherwise a solid cloud of flies would descend on it! The Italian residents of Mogadishu appeared very friendly and cooperative, and clearly depended on the British army to protect them from any hostile attention from their late Somali subjects.

After spending a week in Mogadishu, we took the road again and travelled westward to rejoin the battalion, who were camped at Iscia Baidoa, a centre some 150 miles distant. Here they were recuperating from their recent advances in preparation for the planned entry into Abyssinia. The inhabitants of Baidoa seemed very friendly and cooperative, though perhaps they had little alternative with a full scale armed battalion camped on their doorstep! What a contrast to modern times with the whole country in the hands of quarrelsome tribesmen, and Mogadishu itself no longer a model city, but the centre for warring mobs. We ourselves found the Somalis we encountered reasonably friendly and cooperative, though it must be true that the Somali has a reputation for unreliability, perhaps even cruelty.

I feel that it would be of interest to give a short account of the serious action my battalion had fought prior to their crossing of the Juba river. The Italians had elected to defend against our advance at a place called Bulo Erillo, a little short of the river and with very extensive barbed wire perimeter fencing. After preliminary artillery preparation, the battalion advanced but met up with very strong Italian resistance, rather unexpectedly in front rather than behind their prepared positions. My own company seemed to have been very much in the van, suffering serious losses from machine gun and mortar fire. To make things worse, the Italians set fire to the bush which caused additional confusion in the smoke, and I believe a number of the fallen casualties were roasted or burnt alive.

The company were only able to save the day with a bayonet charge, but after the action I was reliably informed B Company's strength of ten Europeans and 105 Africans had been reduced to only three Europeans and 50 Africans. After the Juba river had been crossed, the Italians retreated as fast as they could back into Abyssinia with the British hot on their heels.

I have often been asked how our West African soldiers got on with their King's African Rifles counterparts, who were immediately distinguished by their blue stockings or puttees. I think, on the whole, very well, though I have heard it said that the KAR thought the West Africans must be cannibals because of their cut faces! As a contrast to this of course the East Africans liked to elongate their earlobes. Africans are great linguists in a pidgin sort of way, and many Gold Coast soldiers picked up a working knowledge of Swahili, and from experiences in POW Camps even some Italian. The West African often referred to their East African counterparts as 'Jambo Jambo men'. This was a reference to the East African native's everyday greeting of 'Jambo – Jambo Bwana' when meeting a European.

12

The Battle of Uaddara and Beyond

After a short stay as Iscia Baidoa, the 2nd Battalion left for the war, passing through Lugh Ferrandi and Dolo and into southern Abyssinia. Close to the frontier we came to Neghelli, from which the Italians had only recently withdrawn. They were at present occupying a line of hills some thirty miles to the north, through which the main road to Addis Ababa ran. This was an extremely strong defensive position, with almost impenetrable forest on the west flank and high mountains on the east confining the main defences to a comparatively narrow front. Our confidence was not exactly improved by knowing that here the Abyssinian Army under Ras Desta had held up the Italians for nearly a year in 1935. It was perhaps only the illegal use of mustard gas that had finally retrieved the position for the Italians.

A broad plain lay between Neghelli and the enemy's positions on the steep and rugged slopes of Uaddara. We were camped some miles short of the enemy in an area of thick orchard bush. In this case, the term orchard bush did not seem inapt at the terrain resembled a landscape of countless fruit trees. The rains were now fully upon us, and while we could keep reasonably dry in our tents, we got very wet on the occasion of our frequent patrols. One patrol lasted two days and provided very rough conditions with continually wet clothes. One would have to retire for the night often wet through, lying on the bare ground, sometimes with and sometimes without a blanket. How one did not suffer from rheumatism in later life will never be known.

As a result of the continual probing by the patrols of the three Gold Coast battalions, the Italians had abandoned their outposts and had withdrawn to their main defensive positions at Uaddara. The Italians had a full division of troops under a General Pralormo. These troops were for the most part native soldiers under Italian officers, but included a high proportion of tough and experienced Eritreans. There were also some irregular detachments and a stiffening of white blackshirts usually kept in reserve. Turning to our own forces, we had been reinforced with a detachment of East African armoured cars, Gold Coast and South African field batteries and the usual Abyssinian irregulars.

The grand attack on Uaddara was scheduled for 4th May, a date I shall not easily forget as it is my birthday! The evening of 3rd May found my company apparently undetected in a position immediately below the slopes leading to the enemy's eastern positions. As usual heavy rain set in, and in consequence we passed a wet and uncomfortable night under the cover of the single blanket that we were allowed to carry with us.

Awake at dawn, we set out with an irregular guide up the steep slope through the forest, and apparently still undetected – at least until one of our nervous force had carelessly discharged his rifle. Soon after that, however, we bumped the enemy who were defending one of the large open glades that were typical of the terrain. We were soon under fire, and it was certainly disconcerting to see leaves falling around us as bullets passed through the trees.

By now all hell had broken out, and the company found itself pinned down for a number of hours by heavy fire from the other side of the glade. As we had advanced some way into the open we suffered a number of casualties, including my Platoon Commander after he had no doubt adopted a rather too upright position! As a result I took over the command of the platoon myself. I believe my predecessor, a Rhodesian called Joss, was eventually evacuated back to base, though I never saw him again. I lost one corporal killed as he fired his Bren gun very close to me, and there were several other casualties. These included one, Awuni Kanjarga, who always carried on his jacket a leather pouch which he boasted contained a very strong juju capable of safeguarding him from death! Unfortunately for him this did not work, and he died. On previous occasions, but not this, we Europeans had been required to black our faces – a fairly wise precaution as the enemy somewhat naturally tried to knock out the white officers or NCOs. My platoon had to provide a burial party the next morning.

During the course of the engagement, a detachment of East African armoured cars appeared on the scene, and indeed, immediately across our front. These were much heavier armoured vehicles than those already described, and were the products of the Nairobi railway workshops. They were immediately successful in knocking out several of the machine gun nests that had been holding us up. Unfortunately, disaster then struck. The Italians had brought up, unbeknown, a 65mm gun, and with this they knocked out two of the armoured cars at point blank range. These caught fire in our sight, and I believe that at least five of the occupants were killed or burnt to death – not a pleasant sight.

By this time the situation seemed to be approaching a stalemate, with my company still pinned down and unable to advance across the open glade. However, one of the other companies had worked round the enemy's left flank, causing them to withdraw, and as a result we were able to advance ourselves. Nightfall was close at hand and we were able to partake of some rations, including a large and very acceptable tot of rum. With the dark the company formed an old-fashioned square, with all the lower ranks facing outwards in firing position. Several volleys were fired during the night, but they were in all probability false alarms, as we found in the morning the enemy had withdrawn from the immediate vicinity. The enemy's Breda machine guns were continually heard both night and day. Their slow and measured double phut-phut was so different from the long salvos from our own Bren guns.

The battle went on for a day or two, with the other two battalions meeting the stiffest resistance on the left flank. Gradually, however, the enemy abandoned their strong positions and started to melt away. No doubt the news of Addis Ababa having fallen behind them on 21st April must have cost them the loss of a lot of morale. A few days later, my company were again waiting overnight to attack another enemy position at the crack of dawn. It must be confessed that, rather to my relief, we found next morning that the enemy had again melted away overnight. The forest here was particularly dense, and I recollect one officer remarking that it reminded him of Ashanti.

During the course of the Battle of Uaddara, and in the subsequent advance through Adola, Hula and Uondo, thousands of demoralised Italian native troops surrendered or were captured with, of course, large quantities of equipment, sometimes indeed to very small advance parties of our troops.

The rains were now fully upon us and road conditions became increasingly chaotic. Sometimes our lorries could make only a mile or two a day, and troops were kept fully occupied digging vehicles out and corduroying the tracks in front of them.

Moving away from the forest country we reached much higher ground, particularly around Hula and Uondo, with an altitude of over 10,000 feet. Camping at night at these heights could be extremely cold, though we had by now been reunited with our tents. The countryside here contained much open grassland, with woods and spinneys, with lots of cattle and horses grazing and many Abyssinians riding about. I would have remarked that these horses were very spirited, but perhaps the prominent spurs worn by the riders might have something to do with this! Game seemed virtually absent, but we did see black and white colobus monkeys in the woods. There were frequent signs of battle along the roads, with broken down vehicles often containing the occasional corpse and the now-familiar sweet smell of death.

By now the supplying of the forward troops had become an administrative headache. While, initially, the NFD had provided a splendid barrier against the enemy reaching the Kenya White Highlands and Nairobi, its 300 miles of tracks, coupled with the appalling roads in southern Abyssinia, were providing substantial transport difficulties. Apart from our important arms and fuel requirements, rations had to be different for the Europeans and African personnel.

I have two reminders of the Abyssinian campaign in my possession. One is a red Italian 'money box' grenade (the outer casing only.) and a Marie Theresa dollar. The money box grenades were indeed somewhat toy-like in comparison to the British Mills grenades, and though they exploded very loudly, their fragmentation was rather limited. They were very useful for booby trapping. They were, however, responsible for a very nasty incident when three British officers were killed as a pile of captured grenades was set off accidentally. It was even more unfortunate to record that by that time main action against the enemy had ceased.

We encountered an unusual currency among the Abyssinian irregulars – the Marie Theresa dollar or Thaler. This was a large heavy coin over 1.5 inches in diameter with Marie Theresa's head and always dated 1780. The Abyssinians also had similar coins, though bearing the head of the late Emperor Menelik. I must admit that I thought the Marie Theresa dollar to be a coinage confined to Ethiopia. However, to my surprise, I have since discovered it has been minted ever since Marie Theresa's death, and the date of the coin has been frozen at 1780. I now understand that it has continued to be struck at least into the 1960s and has been utilised in primitive areas of both East and West Africa. Indeed, an old UAC Coaster, John McGavin MC, who was himself in the East African campaign, has told me that in his early days on the Gold Coast he had found one or two Hausa traders in native markets clinking these dollars!

54

Mention of Capt. John McGavin reminds me of the Military Cross he won after the Battle of Uaddara. In the course of a mopping-up operation he pursued the retreating enemy over the high ground of Adola, Hula and Uando with a force of only three platoons and a section of South African armoured cars. By the use of bluff, and in a series of confrontations, he succeeded in capturing a grand total of 254 Europeans and 2,696 Africans with all their war material – in fact the greater part of a division. John McGavin has for some years been the chairman, and now president, of our 2nd West African Infantry Brigade Association.

13

Soddu. South Western Abyssinia

As already described, after leaving Uaddara the going became more and more difficult and, as a result, a large section of the enemy got clean away. It is doubtful, however, that they still represented a very coherent force. With transport and fuel supplies at a premium, it was decided that my company would have to proceed on foot to Soddu, a distance of 200 or more miles. Soddu was an Italian administrative centre some 400 miles to the southwest of Addis Ababa. Luckily some limited transport was available to accompany us, and this made tented accommodation available when we camped for the night.

We marched as much as 25 miles in the day, though 15 miles was more normal. The going was extremely arduous at times, involving climbing up and down mountainsides with some altitudes as high as 9,000 feet. The roads and paths were sometimes a morass, and at other times hard and stony. Usually the transport had gone ahead and prepared camp. Meals were then cooked, camp beds made up, and even a sit round the camp fire with a whisky was attained. I will mention here the subject of 'comforts'. Officers and BNCOs received rations of cigarettes, beer and the odd bottle of whisky together with any mail, when and if conditions allowed. It was always rumoured that a lot of the supplies were retained and drunk at headquarters! The Abyssinian inhabitants cultivated maize and plantains round their grass huts, and corn cobs became a welcome addition to our diet. Also, chickens and potatoes could be bought or bartered for old items of clothes. On our march we frequently encountered abandoned Italian vehicles, sometimes shot up and occasionally containing dead bodies.

On one occasion we spent all day crossing a low-lying plain of orchard bush reminiscent of the Wajir country – very hot and, for once, no rain. Guinea fowl were common in one locality and formed a popular addition to the pot. We reached by nightfall a largish river whose brown flood waters we thought best to boil before drinking. We eventually arrived at Soddu about 15th June 1941 with our feet no worse for the long walk.

While at Soddu my company was detailed to march into the mountains to accept the surrender of a large band of Italians camped near the Omo river, but several days' march away. They were rumoured to be half starved and menaced by decidedly unfriendly Abyssinian irregulars. These troops were the remnants of General Pralormo's army whom we had previously encountered at Uaddara, and the General was said to be still with them. We were issued with iron rations for the march and one blanket only, again rather inadequate protection for the cold wet nights on the mountains.

This march gave us much insight into the life of the local Abyssinian people. Chiefs sent their subjects with gifts of chickens, eggs, potatoes, beans and local beer, and one very important chief donated a bullock, to the delight of the African soldiers. We Europeans were offered accommodation at night in native huts, but this proved rather a mixed blessing as a lot of insect life was present! It was interesting to find that the natives, like the Swiss, communicated with one another, and from hill to hill, by 'hollering', and we could hear them announcing our approach as we advanced. I have avoided using the term yodelling.

It took us two or three days to reach the vicinity of the Italians' camp. The going was terribly hard at times, up and down steep paths which were often just water courses, as it usually rained several times a day. After reaching the top of a hill we invariable seemed to be faced by a sharp descent into a valley with further ascents still to the front. After toiling up one long slope, we were presented with a particularly breathtaking view. Below us lay the plain where the Italians were camped, but in the distance was range after range of rugged mountains towering up into the sky.

Bringing back the thousand or so Italian soldiers, mostly Europeans, was a rather daunting prospect. Many were in a poor way medically and badly nourished, as the local inhabitants had apparently refused to supply them with food, and some had been living off their mules as they died off. One Italian had his mule with him on our march, but he eventually had to shoot it when it could go no further. One Italian, unable to walk, was devotedly carried by four of his companions, I presume all the way. I found myself at the tail of the long line and had to be really brutal with the stragglers, as, if left behind, they could have expected short shrift from the Abyssinians. Rations reached us before we made camp, and I must have been truly hungry as I recollect eating two tins of corn beef, one after the other!

After the Italians had been safely brought back to Soddu, we experienced more walking, i.e. escorting a large number of prisoners to a centre about 60 miles towards Addis, where they could be more reasonably transported to the capital by lorry. We found the Italian prisoners invariably docile and friendly, but they tended to suffer from many tropical complaints and would give way at times to hysterical outbursts. We Europeans, that is the English not the Italians, now had the advantage of mules to ride, but I generally found it more congenial to walk. In camp one night, we were woken by the violent thrashing about of the tethered mules. A lion had entered the camp.

While the local Abyssinian mules were reasonably comfortable to ride, the big Italian field battery mules could be really stubborn. They had one pace which was slightly quicker than the speed of the marching column. No amount of discouragement or sawing at the mouth would make them walk slightly slower.

Meanwhile, in Soddu we had a reasonably comfortable mess with accommodation in buildings. Rations were now quite good, but while cigarettes were plentiful, there was a shortage of drinks. My skill at bridge improved with nightly games in the mess. A 15-minute each way rugby game between two battalions was a tiring experience, no doubt on account of the altitude.

14

Addis Ababa, Harar and British Somaliland July to October 1941

Early in July orders were received for me to escort a convoy of lorries carrying prisoners to Addis Ababa, afterwards to await the arrival there of the company. I have retained very little recollection of the journey, except for passing through what appeared to be a miniature lake district. On arrival in Addis, and having delivered the prisoners into camp, I had a week to wait before the company itself arrived. As I found two of my friends there on leave, a convivial time was assured. We were able to stay in a rather inferior hotel, though with rooms with running water, etc. at only 1/- a day, one could not really grumble.

Addis was, and presumably still is, a large native town, but with many imposing Italian buildings often standing in groves of eucalyptus trees. The rainy season still continued, and at an altitude of 8,000 feet the climate was cool. Shops were generally short of supplies, though we were able to get good meals of steak, chips, etc. as well as the usual pasta at cafés often run by friendly Greeks.

When the full company did arrive in Addis, I, with an officer, Bill Vincent, took over control of a large prisoner-of-war camp (Europeans). We did not have particularly fine quarters, but there were certain perks – we each had a small Fiat car to run about in, we had the daily services of a barber and there were two skilled chefs to do the cooking for the two of us. These chefs had previously been in charge of restaurants in Milan and Asmara in Italian Eritrea, or so they said. There was plenty of garlic in the meat courses and brandy in the sweets! I read in an old letter home that I had entertained the other BNCOs to dinner one night. The menu was soup, hors d'oeuvre, spaghetti, chicken and a fine cake decorated with strawberries for the sweet.

The Italian prisoners were friendly and well-behaved, though they would escape for short periods, presumably to visit ladies in the town, and possibly with the connivance of our African sentries. Those selected as interpreters, clerks or cooks were particularly privileged. Things were very quiet in Addis during the day, though at night there was usually some sort of a racket going on with odd bursts of gunfire. We certainly made no attempts to find out what it was all about.

On one occasion I marched my platoon to the railway station for the task of escorting a large party of prisoners of war on the train to Diredawa some 250 miles distant. This railway system appeared comparatively well run, and it had always been important in uniting the land-locked Abyssinia to the sea at Djibouti in French Somaliland. The farming areas petered out after about 60 miles, and we then passed through typical 'Mamoba' country for most of the rest of the way. A very prominent feature was the gorge of the Awash river, and we stayed close to a hotel there both coming and going. The Awash bridge had previously been the scene of some spirited action during the war, but I was very interested in the river, which was known to disappear into the extremely remote and inhospitable Danakil Desert without ever reaching the sea. The inhabitants of the Danakil, though little known, have a reputation for hostility and cruelty. I believe only Wilfred Thesiger has much knowledge of them.

Early in August the battalion left Addis, and we set out by convoy for the large town of Harar which, like Diredawa, was on

Addis Ababa
August 1941

The author – 1941

the eastern frontier. By now the war in Abyssinia was almost over except for some mopping up required at Gondar in the far west. The time was now approaching for us to leave East Africa and Harar was a centre on the way to the coast.

The company arrived in Harar at the beginning of September 1941, and we stayed for about a month. We were again in charge of a large prisoner-of-war camp. Harar proved quite a pleasant place with an equable climate, nice buildings and some shops in the European (Italian) quarter. The native town is walled, and dominated by the residence of the Duke of Harar over which, of course, flew again the red, green and gold Ethiopian flag.

In Harar we lived in the best accommodation to date, i.e. a pleasant bungalow with large bedrooms, bathrooms, etc. and we were even able to take our evening drinks on a spacious veranda with splendid views over the surrounding mountains. Moreover, the rainy season was coming to an end and all types of fruit and vegetables, both European and African were available. In the prison-of-war camp I was Acting Quartermaster and after rising early to draw rations, I had most of the rest of the day spare. During the last few months we had ample opportunity to purchase some of the prisoners' more attractive possessions, e.g. binoculars, watches, shotguns and cameras. A lot of the Italians had rather surprisingly very expensive cameras, but I seemed to miss out in obtaining a Contax or a Leica. Some of us Europeans acquired small Italian revolvers usually Birettas and sometimes handsomely carved.

Early in October we were on the move again towards the Horn of Africa and British Somaliland for eventual embarkation at the capital, Berbera. From the highlands of Abyssinia, the road dropped sharply to the Somaliland plain at the Marda Pass. Earlier in the war a company of the Black Watch, of all people, held up a considerable force of Italians here for some days before making an ultimate withdrawal through the port of Berbera. Later in the war, the Italians in turn had unsuccessfully tried to hold up the Nigerians at this same spot.

Pending our departure the battalion camped at Mandera, some 20 miles from Berbera, for about a week until shipping was available at Berbera. We were now back in the hot, dry thornbush country, but with views over forbidding-looking hills in the distance. We were camped close to a large dry river bed, which one day suddenly came down in flood, no doubt as the result of a heavy storm in the hills. At the time I was out walking with my Italian shotgun on the opposite bank of the river and got rather a surprise when I had to wade through quite deep water to regain our camp

15

Return to West Africa

We sailed from Berbera in late October 1941. In a letter home I referred to Berbera as one of the least attractive capitals of the British Empire, though I am sure our army personnel would use more lurid terms than that. The presence in the harbour of a number of large ocean-going dhows that had sailed here from India and obscure ports on the Persian Gulf did, however, provide a little distinction. The battalion embarked on a somewhat venerable liner of the Anchor Line with the improbable name of the *Nea Hellas*. That this title allowed itself to be the subject of unflattering remarks by the troops can well be imagined. After we had settled our African troops on their mess decks, we officers and NCOs descended on the bars with some alacrity. Not for a long time had we sampled cold Australian lager and large gin and tonics! The food and living quarters as compared with the *Reino del Pacifico*, however, proved decidedly second-rate, though the era of the 'dry' troopship was still not with us.

From Berbera we called at Aden to add a few other ships to our convoy. We were not allowed ashore, but apart from missing the experience of stepping on to Asian soil, I am sure we did not miss much. What does stick in my mind, though, was the searing heat of our passage through the Red Sea on our way to Mombasa. With the whole ship blacked out at night time, it was only possible to endure the smoke rooms shirtless and with a large towel to mop one's self. To sleep on deck at night was almost essential. We were anchored at Mombasa for nearly a week, but we spent most of the time in the local bars rather than exploring further afield.

From Mombasa to Durban temperatures gradually reduced, and ashore in Durban we found weather conditions reasonably equitable, with warm days alternating with others with a bitterly cold wind. We left the ship at Durban and spent a fortnight on shore at Clarewood Transit Camp, some ten miles out of town. This gave us the opportunity to get to know Durban, though lack of funds kept us in the camp bar on some nights. I twice went to the races in Durban without much success, though I was very surprised to see the heavy gambling that went on. The rail bookmakers seemed to be mainly dealing with £5 notes, a sum of money not so common in those days.

We sailed again for West Africa on the 15th November and struck lucky again by boarding a rather ancient but still fairly luxurious Orient liner – the *Ormonde*. First class food and excellent service and accommodation. We stopped for four days at Capetown and were able to spend quite a lot of time ashore. One of the main attractions of course was to take the cable car to the top of Table Mountain to see the impressive views over the city and surrounding countryside. At that time, one of the most popular gastronomic features of Capetown was Del Monico's, a large restaurant done out in the Moorish style where one sat under the stars twinkling in an artificial sky above. There was a similar establishment in Durban named the Playhouse. Both restaurants were noted for their mixed grills. Apart from the local 'Castle' lager, the most popular drink in South Africa was Cape Brandy, very cheap but best taken with ginger ale.

While at Durban we found ourselves berthed next to the battleship *The Prince of Wales*. The vessel was busy loading stores for the Far East, and there was great activity all around it and much to-ing and fro-ing of army and naval personnel. It is very

66

St. Andrew's Night, 1941

Atlantic Ocean

——◆——

Saint Andra's Nicht Dinner

——◆——

SOME HAE MEAT AN' CANNA EAT,
AN' SOME WAD EAT THAT WANT IT:
BUT WE HAE MEAT, AN' WE CAN EAT,
AN' SAE THE LORD BE THANKIT.

——◆——

SOME O' THE THINGS WEE'L HAE—

TWA KINDS O' SOUP—

Meat Bree Cockie Leekie

FUSH—

Salmon Mayonnaise

MANY A NICHT WE'VE MERRY BEEN,
AN' MANY MAIR WE HOPE TAE BE.

ENTREE—

Leeks Ecossaise

HAUD YER WHEEST A WEE; HERE, IT'S COMIN'

" HAIL TAE THE CHIEF "

HAGGIS

FAIR FA' YER HONEST SONSY FACE,
GREAT CHIEFTAIN O' THE PUDDIN' RACE.

JINTS—

A Muckle Sirloin o' Beef

Bakit Haum

MON, SIC A DINNER.

Bubbly Jock Roastit
wi' thairm an' stuffin'

Bakit, Boiled an' Snow Tatties
Green Peas

THE PRUIF O' THE PUDDIN'S THE PREEIN O'T.

Grosit Tairt Tremlin Tam

Shortbread
Vanilla Cream Ices

ANITHER COORSE—

Scotch Woodcock

SEAS ATWEEN US BRAID HAE ROARED
SYN AULD LANG SYNE.

DEOCH-AN-DORUIS.

67

sad to recall that within a few weeks *The Prince of Wales*, together with the *Repulse*, was sunk with great loss of life off Singapore.

From Capetown we had un uneventful voyage to Takoradi, and only one event springs to mind. The ship gave us a wonderful dinner on St Andrew's night, and I still have the printed menu, which is illustrated on the previous page.

The return of the regiment was greeted with great enthusiasm at Takoradi and throughout the Gold Coast, and several triumphant parades were made to show the flag. I remember being entertained on the day of our arrival in the mess of the 4th battalion, who had been left in charge of affairs during the brigade's absence in East Africa. On the wall of the mess was displayed the 'Churchillian' notice:

'We also serve who only sit and drink'

Table Mountain, Cape Town

16

On Leave and Back to Civilian Life

After only a day or two back on the Coast, I, with a party of ten others, left for leave in the United Kingdom. First from Takoradi to Freetown on the *New Northland*, a small steamer imported from the Canadian Lakes to provide a coastal service for the army between Nigeria and Bathurst in the Gambia.

On arrival at Freetown, we experienced a typical army delay which involved us spending three weeks ashore at Wilberforce Camp sited on a high spot overlooking the town. While this position had certain attractions, the standard of food and other amenities was not to be recommended. I recollect on one day being faced by a lunch consisting of a plate of plain boiled rice and a bar of chocolate! We were, however, able to visit the somewhat dubious cafés in the town for more adequate meals. The Cotton Tree Café was one of the most popular and, as its name suggests, it was in the square dominated by the large silk cotton tree that presented quite a landmark in Freetown. Life tended to be boring at Wilberforce Camp. There were no bridge players and I spent a lot of time playing brag, sometimes known as poor man's poker.

At long last we sailed from Freetown on the *Almanzora*, a ship of the Royal Mail Line. This was at last a real 'trooper', with, to our disappointment, no alcoholic drinks. Entirely unescorted we appeared to sail straight away into mid-Atlantic, clearly with the object of avoiding all normal shopping routes. Judging by the cold weather we experienced, we may well have approached Iceland during the course of the voyage. No evidence of the enemy was experienced at any time, either in the air or on the sea, and we eventually sailed safely into Glasgow, there to be bombarded with snowballs from dockers on the quay!

Leave spent at home at Ross-on-Wye lasted only six weeks, though the odd visit to London livened things up a bit. Early in March I was ordered to travel to a transit camp at Oxford to await further instructions. Oxford proved to be an attractive town with pleasant hotels and pubs, and I was just settling down nicely when, after only three days, I was given orders to move. I may say that I found this a little unlucky, as many people had found themselves waiting weeks in such camps.

A long train journey through the night brought me again to Glasgow to embark at once at Greenock. This time it was another Royal Mail liner, the *Alcantara*, which had been fully fitted out as an armed merchant cruiser. Things were not too bad, though for the first time we were on mess decks and sleeping in hammocks. Rather surprisingly I found these quite comfortable as ordinary mattresses were placed in them. We had reasonable food and played a lot of bridge. We were subject to naval discipline and took our turn on watch.

The *Alcantara* was one ship in a very large convoy clearly bound for the Middle East. There were about twenty large troop carrying liners guarded by a very strong escort which included an aircraft carrier, a cruiser and a number of destroyers and corvettes which usually sailed on our flanks. Watching the movements of all these ships around us each day was of absorbing interest. Activity always centred around the aircraft carrier, from which Swordfish and other planes were continually taking off and returning, both for reconnaissance and exercises. On occasions planes dragged drogues to provide artillery practice for the smaller warships. As with all wartime convoys, the possibility of submarine interference had always to be anticipated. The more vulnerable ships in the centre of the convoy would change course as one, in a series of different length zig zags, and the progress of the convoy would be measured by the speed of the slowest ship.

The convoy subsequently called in at Freetown, as all convoys did in those days, to take on coal, water or oil. Freetown of course held a very strategic position on the west coast of Africa, and a number of small warships were stationed there to patrol the seas for submarines. As the Mediterranean was a dangerous sea route at that time, most convoys destined for the Middle or Far East used the route by the Cape. On arrival at Freetown we again boarded the *New Northland*, but on this occasion we were confined on board for nine days in the harbour without any chance of going ashore. There was no beer on board but plenty of Canadian Club whisky and Canadian cigarettes. The main drawback was the heat at night when all the portholes were blacked out. Once on the way, we reached our destination Takoradi within a day or two.

Back in the Gold Coast, we found the battalion camped out on the Accra Plains close to the small town of Akuse on the Volta river. These are grassy plains with some incidence of low trees and shrubs, which provided grazing for small herds of the native coastal cattle which must have been fairly tolerant of the tsetse fly and subsequent trypanosomiasis.

No sooner had I reported to the battalion than I was told that I was to leave the army and to rejoin my department who needed their members back in the interests of increased wartime food production. Perhaps, strangely, I did not find this idea at all congenial. After two and a half years in the army I had become accustomed to military life and all my friends were there. Moreover, I was due to attend an OCTU (Officer Training Course) shortly, so I also missed out on promotion. I was particularly aggrieved not to have heard of this before as otherwise, rather than six weeks of leave, I would have had my normal quota of three or four months, would probably have travelled on a more comfortable ship as a civilian, and would not have left a lot of clothes behind. An interview with the Battalion Commander, however, proved unproductive, and I returned rather reluctantly to 'civvy street'.

Just one memory of the camp at Akuse – a good party one evening with our Regimental Sergeant Major, a Scot called McKechan, singing every verse of the 'Ball of Kerremuir'. He was from the Black Watch, had a very large handlebar moustache and a great capacity for whisky. His home was on North Uist in the Outer Hebrides, and he maintained that when he arrived back in the United Kingdom on leave, it took him several days' travel to reach home.

After Akuse, I moved into a government rest house in Accra to await further instructions. This at least was luxury – a refrigerator, electric light, etc., not to mention proximity to the club. I recruited a cook and steward and acquired stores for my new station, which proved to be Koforidua in the Eastern Province, though only about 60 miles from Accra.

17

Koforidua. May to October 1942

Koforidua was, and presumably still is, an important town in the eastern region of the Gold Coast. It was on the main railway line linking Accra and Kumasi in Ashanti. Koforidua lay within the forest belt, and being situated in rather a bowl, might be considered a hot station. The main rainy season developed in May and June, bringing much cooler weather necessitating the use of a blanket on the bed at night.

At the time of my stay in Koforidua, there would have been some forty Europeans stationed there. The government officers lived on the 'Ridge', while the commercial representatives lived in the town, often over their stores. I should explain that the term 'Ridge' is the area set aside for the bungalows of the senior government officers. While this area would be close to the town, it would be set at the highest point that the local terrain would allow. If there was no higher ground, however, the area would still be known as the 'Ridge'!

As the headquarters of the eastern region, the Provincial Commissioner was stationed at Koforidua and occupied the Residency, a dwelling of some style. As was the case at other centres, officers stationed here represented the police, agricultural and forestry departments, education, the Public Works Department, a magistrate and of course the resident District Commissioner.

The commercial representatives included those of the United Africa Company, G. B. Ollivants, Busi and Stephenson, Cadbury Fry and the French companies.

Returning to civilian life involved a return to the etiquette that still persisted in government circles. While printed visiting cards went out with the war, it was necessary to sign the senior government officer's book on arriving at or leaving a station. The book was always placed in a small covered shelter at the front of the big man's bungalow. Care was always necessary at arranging seating at a dinner party. Woe betide you if you did not place the senior lady at the host's right at the end of the table, and the same of course to the hostess at the other end. After dinner nobody should leave until the senior lady did. Only a political officer would be able to display a Union Jack flag at his residence or, for that matter, on his car.

While I was resident in Koforidua for only a few months, I occupied no fewer than three bungalows, the best being that of the District Commissioner who was on leave at the time. This DC was James Moxon, who later became well known for staying on in Ghana after his retirement. He then lived at Aburi some twenty miles from Accra, and was so respected by the locals that they made him a chief. In 1969 he wrote a definitive handbook on the Volta River Lake. I believe he now spends half the year at Aburi and half the year in England. At each site I established a garden growing lettuces, tomatoes, runner beans, etc. and as if my staff of two were not enough, I also recruited a garden boy at 15/- a month. However, he was also responsible for collecting firewood for which my cook would have charge me 6d a day. I did not acquire a car for a month or two, but then purchased a rather elderly 26HP Vauxhall with a capacity of little more than 20 miles to the gallon. We were of course severely rationed for petrol and I remember, of all odd things, actually walking to the office and freewheeling the car down dangerous hills with somewhat dodgy brakes!

Instead of dealing with food production, I was for the time being in the Cooperative division of the department and had the imposing title of Assistant Registrar of Cooperative Societies (ARCS for short). The department had encouraged a considerable number of cocoa cooperative societies which, in the eastern region, included three central societies incorporating some 70 primary societies. The supervision of these societies required quite a bit of travelling, with some nights spent away from the station and staying in rest houses. I was also required to handle and pay out quite large sums of money, both for cocoa payments and also where loans and bonuses were required. As much as £2,000 could be handled at one payout, all in small coin denominations – quite a lot of money for those days. While I was always careful to carry my safe keys on my person, it says a lot for the honesty of the population that I was never apprehensive of being waylaid.

During the latter part of my stay in Koforidua, the minor season cocoa crop was picked. Insufficient shipping was available to export all this crop, and as the cocoa farmers could not be left without income, the decision was taken to buy the crop in the normal manner and then destroy it with fire. The cocoa had of course to be of gradable quality. Supervision of this work fell to me and this, of course, was a position of some responsibility, otherwise sharp practice could easily arise.

I should mention here the presence of the West African Research Institute (WACRI) some twenty miles north of Koforidua. Some twenty research officers, mainly Europeans, were stationed here and they of course worked in close association with the Department of Agriculture. One of the chief problems being dealt with at WACRI was the serious cocoa disease known as Swollen Shoot which was spreading ominously through the cocoa areas.

The war effort was being taken fairly seriously in Koforidua and both the ARP and a Homeguard had been established. I did my best to institute some military spirit into the ARP, though it did not seem likely that we should ever be called upon to meet any serious threat in British West Africa! Most imported foodstuffs were still in reasonable supply, with the possible exceptions of butter and potatoes. Yams were a good substitute for the latter of course and, in fact, one could live quite cheaply and adequately 'on the country'. There was plenty of Accra beer and cigarettes, though one had to deal with several stores to get a reasonable supply of whisky. The Governor of the Gold Coast at that time was Sir Arnold Hodson. He was an able and efficient governor, but of parsimonious mind. He kept expenditure down at the Castle and suggested that a European could live adequately on 1/- a day! Expatriates did not agree!

Meanwhile, Koforidua was very lively as far as social life was concerned, there was snooker in the club and with my partner Frankie Bubb of Cadbury's, I played bridge once or twice a week with other Koforidua residents. My cook was capable of producing excellent several course meals when it was my turn for entertaining. In the case of any shortage of knives and forks or crockery, the servants would borrow from neighbouring bungalows, usually I think unbeknown to the rightful owners. There was, however, a little embarrassment when one night, having rather daringly asked the Provincial Commissioner and his wife round to dinner, there was crested silver on the table, obviously from the Residency. Nobody said anything!

In September I learnt that I was to transfer in October to Kumasi in Ashanti and I remember, as a wartime measure, I was required to put the car on the train. A letter home at that time illustrates the helpful and friendly nature of one's neighbours. For three days prior to my departure all meals were provided by friends and compatriots, though I do seem to have squeezed a groundnut party of my own for seven people on the Sunday. While in a tour of duty one might be required to move several times, this was not unduly onerous. Government bungalows had permanent if fairly austere furniture, and what possessions did require moving were soon attended to by the boys.

18

Kumasi. October 1942–March 1944

After leaving Koforidua, I spent the last eighteen months of my tour in Kumasi, the capital of Ashanti and a city second in size only to Accra. There would probably have been some 300 to 400 Europeans in Kumasi in 1942, mostly British, but also a sprinkling of other nationalities – French, Swiss and Greeks in particular. One must also mention the numerous Syrians, Lebanese and Indian traders and the presence of the regiment. Banks, as elsewhere, were represented by the Bank of British West Africa (Lloyds) and Barclays.

Continuing my work with the cocoa cooperatives, my activities in Ashanti were largely confined to the forested areas in the south of the territory. A good network of roads existed throughout, serving the large number of villages that were to be found in the forest. Apart from the roads, the area south of the capital was well served by the railway. While it was in the war interest to use the railway as much as possible, much of my work concerned societies north and west of Kumasi, and there it was necessary to use my own transport, particularly if carrying large sums of money; in fact insurance regulations demanded it. The main cocoa season was now approaching, and this necessitated as much as £6,000 being paid out in a week.

Even by today's standards, the carrying of such large sums of money would have been considered quite formidable, particularly where a young man of comparatively tender years was concerned, and I would indeed have been held responsible for making good any discrepancy. Regarding loans if an application could not be fully supported by sufficient share capital, I might have to inspect cocoa farms to assess their value as security. When talking of cocoa farms, it must be realised that the average cocoa farm was seldom more than one or two acres in extent, and with very irregular shaped borders; though it was true that one farmer might own a number of such farms, and also employ a number of Northern Territory labourers. It was the latter who could be at some risk if a prominent local chief should happen to die. The disappearance of an odd immigrant native could pass unnoticed if he had been selected to accompany a deceased chief to his happy hunting ground! Cocoa was grown under the shade of large forest trees and the farm's boundaries were perhaps only appreciated by the owners themselves.

There were some 60 or 70 primary cocoa societies in Ashanti, grouped under four central societies. Each primary had a paid secretary, and I had under my command a number of junior district African officers. Occasional visits were made by the Head of Department from Accra, one Eric Hay, a Scotsman. He was sometimes referred to as 'Eric or bottle by bottle', but though the reason for this title may have been fairly obvious, he was in actual fact an officer of marked efficiency. Apart from cocoa, we also encouraged our members to assist the war effort by supplying rubber and palm kernels, the former coming mainly from latex-bearing trees and vines growing wild in the forest, and in particular, funtumia elastica.

My duties involved a lot of travelling, with perhaps four or five nights a month staying in government rest houses. Travelling 'on trek' was well worthwhile as it earned larger travelling and mileage allowances. Rest houses differed widely in their amenities and attractiveness, but they did supply a bed and some fairly rudimentary articles of furniture, plus a varying population of bats, mice, lizards, mosquitos and other forms of wild life. Light was provided with one's own Tilley lamp, while the cook managed with a hurricane lamp in his tiny outside kitchen. Catering rest houses became commoner in later years, though even then they were confined to the larger centres. When staying in bush rest houses, the chief often sent round a 'dash' of a chicken, eggs, yams, etc. though it was considered customary to reciprocate with further dashes in kind. A dash, by the way, means a gift or a tip, and was a very widely-used expression all over West Africa. Staying in the vicinity of the gold mines at Konongo, Obuasi and Bibiani allowed visits to the well-equipped mines clubs.

There were, during my tour, six members of the Department of Agriculture stationed in Kumasi. The hospitality of one's fellow officers was well illustrated by my first Christmas in Kumasi. Each member in turn, including myself, gave a large party over the three or four days of holiday and as a result one became a little jaded towards the end of this period, though recovering sufficiently for a new round of parties at the New Year. It was sometimes said about Kumasi that Christmas started each year at the beginning of December and finished at the end of January, though perhaps this was somewhat of an exaggeration.

While by 1943 imported foodstuffs were getting a little harder to find, it was perhaps shortages of petrol, tyres and lorry spares that presented a more serious problem. With some 150,000 tons of cocoa to bring into Kumasi during the main cocoa season transport difficulties were legion, and I was continually badgered by cooperative societies, lorry drivers, etc. to assist in recommending permits to purchase tyres, fuel, etc., and even new vehicles. Apart from those areas served by the railway, the population of the innumerable villages in the bush were dependant on the services of countless 'mammy' lorries, and the accident rates for these vehicles were certainly being increased by the use of bald tyres and lack of spare parts. It is nowadays not always appreciated that after a tyre becomes bald the driver still has several layers of canvas to go through before the final burst!

As may be imagined the club was the centre for social affairs, with much of the entertainment centred on the snooker table. As was the case everywhere else on the Gold Coast no straight snooker or billiards was played – everything was 'volunteer'. 'Volunteer' snooker allows the potting of coloured balls out of sequence which enables much bigger breaks to be made. Regular dances were held at the club on Saturday nights, and usually under the auspices of the Gold Coast police band. Their rendition of the 'Umbrella Man' with a vocal was one of their favourite pieces. Popular dances for the whole community were also held at Prempeh Hall, with both the white and black population in full evening dress and the African ladies in their colourful cottons. The most usual Gold Coast dance was of course the High Life with, 'EVERYBODY, EVERYBODY likes Saturday night' being the most popular refrain.* A sit outside cinema was equally popular with both Africans and Europeans.

With a second Christmas at Kumasi fast approaching, my thoughts increasingly turned to leave. Christmas was again a hectic affair, coinciding with the cool nights and dry hot days of the harmattan, which seemed to add to the Christmas spirit. These conditions caused even heavy furniture to creak and warp. My predecessor, who was named Dobbin, never came back to the Coast. Being torpedoed twice, both going home and attempting

---

*I must mention the time in the evening when comes the announcement – 'the Grand Chain'. With the band increasing the tempo, everyone forms a large circle though continuing to dance in time with the music. In the centre a single dancer holds the stage with a handkerchief at the ready. He or she shimmies around 'threatening' this one or that with the handkerchief. When a 'victim' is finally selected the handkerchief is transferred and the dance goes on. The recipient is of course of the opposite sex, or when I once was the only European to take part, it had to be me.

to return must have been too much for him! Conversely, during my several sea trips during the war, I was lucky not to encounter a single untoward incident with the enemy. In March 1944 I was finally able to get away on leave, after what had proved to be a 24 months' tour of duty.

We sailed from Takoradi for Freetown for the third time on the *New Northland* and supplies of Canadian products were still plentiful. On leaving the Gold Coast, however, we little knew that it would be six full weeks before we eventually reached the UK. At Freetown we quickly transferred to one more large passenger liner, this time the *Queen of Bermuda*. The passengers were mainly civilians, the ship was dry, the accommodation troopshiplike, but the food was not too bad. Unfortunately, the passage was delayed by our being diverted to Gibraltar, where we stayed tied up in the harbour for the best part of three weeks.

It was very boring in board in Gibraltar, and we were only allowed to go on shore once during the whole three weeks. I remember spending many hours playing pontoon with rounds of Coca-cola and other soft drinks. What a predicament! At all hours of the day and night the ship was shaken by depth charges. These were exploded at irregular intervals to discourage limpet mines being attached to hulls of ships in the harbour. A depth charge exploded would apparently spell death to any underwater swimmer in the harbour confines at that time. At long last, on a fine spring day in April our ship arrived once more in the port of Glasgow.

19

Koforidua Again.
October 1944–March 1946

The summer of 1944 was spent very pleasantly on leave in England, and indeed for the normal eighteen weeks' period. My stay of course coincided with the Allies' invasion of Western Europe, so life was full of interest, even if one did feel a little guilty about being out of it all. I might mention here that visits to London were always essential features of home leave, and no visit was complete without a curry lunch at the famous Veeraswamy's in Swallow Street. I usually caused the steward some surprise by requesting extra hot sauce with the Vindaloo! However, good things have to come to an end, and in early October I took a long night's train journey to arrive at Newcastle-on-Tyne at breakfast time. There I embarked at once on a French passenger/cargo boat, the name of which escapes me. We spent a lovely autumn day sailing down the east coast of England and into the Channel with no longer any fear of enemy interference.

Conditions on the French ship were fairly reasonable, and the passengers were mainly civilians bound for various West African ports. I remember arranging with a burly member of the Forestry Department – Frank Harper – to share a table for two in the dining room. We both awarded the French table steward £1 each as a starter tip, with more to come. As a result the food was very good and plentiful, and there was also some excellent Chilean wine. On board was another fellow Coaster, Johnny Forett from G. B. Ollivants, and together we introduced to various interested parties the risky gambling game of 'Farmers Glory', very popular among Herefordshire farmers and sometimes called Slippery Sam. Things did not go quite to plan, and by the time the ship reached Takoradi both Harper and I were penniless, and we were obliged to sneak ashore out of sight of the expectant table steward!

Once more in Korofidua I resumed work with my cocoa societies in the eastern region. I was allocated quite a small bungalow at first, but by February I had moved into a much larger one and indeed, the steward boy, having observed the large expanse of wooden floors to polish, immediately demanded the recruitment of a 'small boy'! I remember fruit bats being very active at night at Koforidua. One seemed to be resident just outside my bedroom window, and it sounded like somebody rhythmically beating a metal sheet with a hammer. A feature of Koforidua was the spectacular flame trees (Poinciana Regina) which flowered in April and May among the bungalows. During my stay in Koforidua I was asked to dinner by George Cansdale of the Forestry Department. He was a great authority on all aspects of wild life in the colony, and in particular the snakes. Later on he became famous in the United Kingdom with his connections with the London Zoo,

The cocoa season was in full swing soon after Christmas, and the price of cocoa had been increased from 7/- to 12/- a load – a load of 60 lbs weight was always the standard measure for weighing cocoa in the Gold Coast. By 1945 the societies' secretaries had become responsible for the payment of all monies, which made my work much simpler, though the risk of losses through dishonest personnel and office bearers must have increased considerably.

It was a stipulation that all ex-patriot government officials should pass an examination in one of the local languages. While there are many locally spoken minor languages and dialects, particularly in the Northern Territories, in the southern half of the country there were four main tongues – Fante in the southern and western regions, Twi in Ashanti, Ga in Accra, and Ewe (pronounced Evé) in Transvolta/Togoland. These languages are not easy for Europeans to learn, and there was indeed not much incentive to do so, as all educated Gold Coasters including all our staff spoke excellent English, and were always at hand to act as interpreters where village meetings were concerned.

I elected to study Fante, and eventually went up to Kumasi to take the examination (oral). Perhaps a word or two in the ear of the African Chief Clerk in our Ashanti office was of considerable assistance, as he appeared to know the examiner quite well! Anyway, I passed without much trouble, and great were the jollifications in the Kumasi club that night.

How different were the conditions obtaining in the East African territories. There, Europeans avoided speaking English with their domestic staff, invariably conversing in Swahili. Swahili, however, is a language spoken over a huge area and is a language, rather like Hausa or even Italian, fairly easy to acquire even if in a 'pidgin' sort of way. In the Gold Coast and Nigeria there are a number of rather complex languages and English is taught in all schools.

A word or two about health may be of interest. West Africa has always had an unenviable reputation for such alarming tropical maladies as malaria, black water fever, sleeping sickness and yellow fever. While the last three are mainly confined to the past, malaria remained an ever-present risk. The main consideration is of course to avoid being bitten by anopheles mosquitoes. Hence the essential use of mosquito nets and long trousers and mosquito boots after the evening bath. The other approach was by the use of prophylactic medicines. When I first arrived in the Gold Coast it was the habit to take a tablet of quinine at the time of the evening 'sundowner'. In the army we progressed to mepacrine, which appeared to be very efficient but produced in time a 'yellow as a guinea' complexion. After leaving the army, I regularly took paludrine. This had no obvious drawbacks and kept me free from fever for the rest of my stay in West Africa. Only on two occasions when on leave did I go down with an attack, and then I had clearly neglected to continue the medication on leave as I had been directed.

Truth to tell, I kept very fit in West Africa and was only inconvenienced by comparatively minor ailments. These included a problem on one occasion with hookworm, a jigger larva in my toe, and the occurrence of a filaria worm which appeared under the skin from time to time in various parts of the body. It was always said that the only way to catch such a pest was when it passed over the eyeball! The Africans living in more primitive places might be subject to much more unpleasant complaints which were most frequently waterborne, e.g. Guinea worm, which produced very nasty sores on the legs, bilharzia and river blindness.

For the maintenance of good health, we were very dependent on the good practices of our servants. All bungalows were equipped with large stone filters through which all drinking water had to be passed after boiling. Salads should always be washed in potassium permanganate.

Despite the fact that we ate plenty of local produce, tummy upsets were rare, and I am sure that our regular use of local foods inured us against such troubles. Later on in the war many Americans came to the colony, and they had almost all their food imported. I am sure they would have been very much more subject to food poisoning if they had departed from imported foods.

The war had occasioned another change in the habits of Europeans. It was observed that white army personnel or crews of ships seemed to ignore with impunity the 'dangerous rays' of the tropical sun. Accordingly, the necessity of wearing solar topees all day became unnecessary and trilby hats seemed quite sufficient.

One of my favourite treks was to stay at a rest house at Mpraeso. This rest house was situated over 1,000 feet up on a scarp above the railway town of Nkawkaw. Approached through an impressive avenue of royal palms, it was a lot cooler than my usual residence and the rest house keeper would if requested make a fire, that is if you could withstand the smoke!

During my service up to date, I had continued to hold the rank of Inspector of Produce, though I had never been called upon to carry out the much simpler tasks of port inspection. I was now recommended for promotion to the post of Agricultural Officer, though I would first have to attend a year's course at the School of Tropical Agriculture in Trinidad after my next leave. I accordingly sailed for home on a new Elder Dempster ship, the two original mail boats, the *Accra* and the *Appapa*, having both been torpedoed and sunk in the war.

A Forest Road

20

A Year in Trinidad. 1946–1947

Early in September 1946 I sailed from the now defunct London East India Docks en route for Trinidad on the cargo ship, the *Adviser*. This vessel was owned by the Harrison Line, which in those days owned a small fleet of ships trading with British Guiana and the Caribbean. The *Adviser* carried about sixty passengers, but conditions were not very comfortable, e.g. six to a cabin, a very small bar and limited deck space. Among the passengers were eight young Cambridge undergraduates also destined for the School of Tropical Agriculture and subsequent Colonial Agricultural Service – also the College Dean.

After some rough weather, conditions improved and became very hot. The ship was a slow one and it took 13 days to reach our one and only port of call – Bridgetown, Barbados. At that time there were no tie-up facilities and we anchored offshore, but were able to spend the best part of two days on land while the ship was discharging cargo. Swimming at the Aquatic Club was very pleasant, and one night we stayed out until the early hours at a swinging nightclub known as the Club Morgan. It must have been a good party as I remember slipping off the gangway into the sea on our return to the ship. We also travelled through the cane fields one evening to have dinner with a schoolmaster we had met on the ship. This reminded me that there is a difference between West

Africa and the West Indies in the hiring of domestic servants. In West Africa nearly all the servants are male, while in the West Indies they are usually female, and if a household does employ a male servant, he is grandly referred to as the butler.

We arrived at Port of Spain, Trinidad, on 20th September after 18 hours' passage from Barbados. From here we took a taxi to the college, situated at St Augustines, some nine miles out of town. I was at first given a room in the main students' block, but probably because of my mature years I found the proximity of thirty or so noisy young West Indians somewhat unsettling, to say the least! However, after moving into a small adjacent building, I settled down and got on well with all the younger students, though my habit of taking a siesta in the afternoons appeared to surprise them.

As the term did not start until early October, there was not too much to do for a while. Meals were taken in the main hostel, and for the first time I encountered the local vegetables – tanias, eddoes and dasheens, all farinaceous and the equivalent of the cassava and yam in West Africa. There was a bar selling mainly beer and soft drinks. Rum was very cheap but other spirits were expensive.

My work at the college was not unduly onerous. Lectures were mainly in the mornings, and there were frequent afternoon expeditions to sites of agricultural interest – sugar cane plantations and factories, livestock centres, etc. To visit the bustling capital of Port of Spain we used the roving taxis, large American limousines which differed very much in age and smartness. Some of us joined the Country Club. There was not exactly a colour bar at the club, but full members had to be reasonably well-connected and preferably not too dark of countenance. At weekends we visited Marracas Bay where there was excellent bathing and a splendid view over the rocky islands known as the Bocas. Here I first saw pelicans diving steeply into the sea after fish. Our neighbouring town had the improbable name of Tunapuna and possessed an up-to-date cinema. However, as Tunapuna was the centre of a large

Imperial College of Tropical Agriculture, Trinidad

East Indian population, the films were normally of Indian origin.

I was soon prevailed upon to play rugby. Apart from the college there were I remember only three other teams on the island – one in Port of Spain, and one each at the oil companies based at Pointe à Pierre and Port Fortin. To make up additional fixtures, such contests as the Over-30s versus the Under-30s were arranged. I was of course in the former category, and in fact I found that my ankles had difficulty in standing up to the pressure. Pointe à Pierre included among its rather dubious attractions the unusual Pitch Lake.

A great feature of Trinidad, and to a lesser extent on most of the other islands, was the cult of the calypso. There were a number of calypso bands on Trinidad, and at the time of my visit the greatest star of all was Lord Kitchener. I am a little surprised to see that there still is a Lord Kitchener in Trinidad. It cannot possibly be the same one, so perhaps it is a title awarded annually? The great attribute of the calypso vocalist is to be able to sing

89

about anyone or any event in a humorous way at a moment's notice. As an example, a description of me at the college Christmas party:

> Exactly why Lord Leeds is here,
> I cannot really say,
> But he has already been appointed,
> Tunapuna's D of A,
> As well as Sergeant Major,
> Of the college police,
> But in his rum his water
> he really should increase.

D of A of course means Director of Agriculture, and the remark about the Sergeant Major refers to an incident when I drilled the college watchman somewhat late at night after a rugby match! Peculiarly this ditty was sung in perfect calypso style by an English lecturer whose name I think was Dale. He was also at Wye College, and later joined the Ministry of Agriculture at Wolverhampton.

The great event of the year in Trinidad was of course CARNIVAL. This was held after Lent, and jollifications would go on non-stop, and I mean non-stop, for two or three days and nights. On the initial morning I was in Port of Spain with other college students well before 8 o'clock watching the gaily adorned processions of bands and vehicles passing through the streets. Rum was king at the carnival, and I remember that I did not return to the college until the next morning. We students occasionally visited the pretentious Queen's Park Hotel which overlooked the Queen's Park Savannah where horse racing takes place and cricket Test Matches are played. At night time the grounds are spectacularly lit up by glow worms. Turning to quieter matters, I usually took a walk every evening through the adjacent rice fields where the frogs kept up a persistent lullaby, very different from the harsh croaking of West African frogs.

I chose as the subject for my thesis at college a study of the agriculture of the Northern Range which provided the highest altitude on the island, though this was little more than 3,000 feet above sea level. The chief problem there was one of soil erosion. As in many other tropical countries, shortage of food farming space had encouraged farmers to cultivate further and further up hill features, and as a result the subsequent shifting cultivation and cut-and-burn farming had caused considerable soil degradation.

The event of the year for the 'English' college student was a fortnight's visit to British Guiana (now Guyana). We sailed to the capital, Georgetown, by rice boat. I am not sure whether rice was exported from Trinidad to B.G. or vice versa, as both countries grew rice! It is possible that the lecturer who selected this form of transport might have had his tongue in his cheek – the rice boats are small, and the seas between Trinidad and South America notoriously choppy. The food served for the evening meal consisted of rather oily salt pork, and I believe for the only time in my life I really felt seasick.

Ashore in the capital, Georgetown, we were put up at a small hotel with the rather unimposing name of the Woodbine. Georgetown was a busy city with, in the old Dutch Quarter, beautiful wooden houses then occupied by the better-off part of the population. B.G., as the country was usually referred to, had a densely populated coastline, some ten to twenty miles wide where large acreages of sugar cane were grown, mainly by large companies. Much of this land was actually below sea level, and whose polders dated back to the days of Dutch occupancy. B.G. was often referred to as Bookers Guiana, as the firm of Bookers monopolised most of the trade in the country, just as had the United African Company in British West African colonies.

The interior of B.G. had few roads, and access was mainly confined to the great rivers or by air. The Indian inhabitants, and by this I am not referring to the East Indians, were sparsely spread and as a result there was little disturbance of the forest. If the forest was felled, however, and the thick layers of fallen leaves exhausted, the soils quickly became unfertile. B.G. was however noted for one tree indigenous only to the country – the greenheart. This timber was extremely durable for ship building and harbour works. Only in the north were conditions suitable for cattle farming. Two features of B.G. which I sadly missed seeing were the 9,000 foot Mount Roraima in the north (Conan Doyle's Lost World?) and the famous Kaieteur Falls on the Venezuelan frontier, reputed to be five times the height of Niagara and approachable only by air, apparently a terrifying experience. Are the Kaieteur Falls and the Angel Falls one and the same?

Perhaps the most interesting portion of our tour was a trip up the Essiquibo river by ferry as far as the settlement of Bartica, some 200 miles north of Georgetown. It is there that another great river, the Cayuni, joined the Essiquibo. We stayed the night at the

Planting rice, Trinidad

92

local hotel in Bartica and we were regaled for dinner with what we thought was a chicken dish. Very nice too, though afterwards we were told that it was iguana lizard. The night was made discordant by the howler monkeys in the forest and the barking of what must have been a very large population of local pie dogs.

We were advised not to bathe in the rivers as shoals of bloodthirsty piranha fish abound, and electric eels can be formidable opponents. The Essiquibo is several miles wide at its mouth, and river traffic is dense as far as Bartica at least. River traffic varies from small canoes to large passenger-carrying ferries. Could some of the crews of outboard-driven launches we saw be the famous 'pork knockers' in search of diamonds? No doubt however such activities occurred much further upstream. We also stayed the night at a small town on the coast called Adventure. On the estuary we bathed from the shore, though we found the water tea brown from washed-down detritus from the interior, and this effect prevailed quite far out to sea. We were also able to launch up part of the much smaller Demerara river.

After successfully completing my examinations I was sent with another student to Grenada to survey cocoa plantations on the island for Swollen Shoot disease, a malady now becoming widespread in West Africa. We flew to Grenada and stayed in lodgings in the capital of St George's. Our digs overlooked the beautiful bay in which, in later years, we anchored in the Geest banana boats. Tied up along the quay were usually a number of ocean-going schooners which sailed between the different islands carrying passengers, small livestock, foodstuffs and all manner of goods. Unlike the Gold Coast, cocoa growing in Grenada was largely a plantation crop, and each day the local Department of Agriculture arranged for us to visit several of these plantations for inspection. The day's proceedings, however, were usually brought to a sudden conclusion about 11 o'clock, at the invitation of the planter to attend 'breakfast'. This was a fully-fledged meal accompanied by rum. We found no Swollen Shoot but saw plenty of Witch's Broom, a fungous disease fairly widespread on cocoa in South America but not known in West Africa.

Grenada was and it still is of course famous as a Spice Island, producing as it did quantities of nutmegs, mace, ginger, turmeric and other exotics both for export and local consumption. We were able to tour the island in some detail, including such memorable sites as the Grand Etang Lake and the famous Morne de Sauteurs at the northern tip of the island. It was there in 1651 that the last remaining Caribs escaped the French by leaping to their deaths from the cliffs. Nearby is the sparsely populated Levera beach, from which a whole flotilla of small uninhabited islands can be seen, with such interesting names as Kicking Jenny, Les Tantes, Green and Sandy Islands and Ile Ronde. Further out looms the larger bulk of Grenada's sister island, Cariacou. We also of course bathed on the famous Grand Anse beach, two miles of perfect golden sands. While I was able to visit a lot more West Indian islands later in my life, I have always considered Grenada my favourite.

I, together with the other English students, returned to England by Pan Am airways, but stopped off for a week in New York. Apart from visiting such important landmarks as the Empire State Building, Macy's stores, etc., I am afraid to say that a lot of our time was spent in local bars and night spots, including the famous Jack Dempsey's bar on Broadway. Leaving La Guardia airport we flew back over the Atlantic to the United Kingdom with stops only at Gander in Newfoundland and Dublin. There was a worrying incident at the airport. My ticket was nowhere to be found and the authorities refused point blank to allow me on the plane without it. However, with the financial assistance of the other students, I raised the money for another ticket, to be claimed back later.

I have several times referred to rum in the foregoing pages. Barmen in the West Indies are adept at mixing rum punches. Apart from the rum, the essential ingredients are plenty of crushed ice, the juice from freshly cut limes, angostura bitters and the right amount of sugar syrup. Also, perhaps, a dusting of nutmeg. When I was in Trinidad the shorter rum swizzle was also an important drink, but it seems to have gone out of fashion nowadays. The price of rum and rum drinks varies from very cheap indeed in low rum shops in Port of Spain to very expensive in such swish hotels as Sandy Lane in Barbados.

Most of the rum used in the United Kingdom, and of course in the Navy, comes from Jamaica. After I had got used to the lighter rum of Trinidad and other islands, I found these Jamaican rums too dark and strong tasting for my palate. Rums from the other West Indian islands and South America all have individual tastes and flavours and vary in colour from white to very dark brown. None, however, is so dark and strong tasting as the Jamaican variety. For making rum punches in England my selection would be the Barbados rum, Mountgay.

A great tradition of the West Indies is the widespread use of very hot sauces which the locals use at almost all meals. Unaccustomed users should beware as only very small quantities are advisable. A well-known Grenadian brand illustrates on the bottle a mule with a raised tail and the caption, 'Hot going in and hot coming out'! Hot pepper sauce is made from chilli peppers, onions, tomatoes and vinegar, but mainly chillies. It seems to keep for ever. We have a bottle of hot sauce that has been in our fridge for several years and is still in perfect condition. That, incidentally, came from Barbados and perhaps it improves with keeping.

The climate of Trinidad was tropical, but I never found the conditions to be unduly hot. Living in the college grounds was very healthy with no incidence of mosquitoes or malaria. I have recollection of only one insect pest, the Jack Spaniard. This was a wasp rather similar to its European counterpart, but of a much more aggressive nature. Their nests were common and there was one under the college swimming pool's diving board. To sit on this risked a serious winged assault.

It was sugar and cocoa that made Trinidad rich, and later oil became very important. The population of the island was divided almost equally between the East Indian and the African origin factions – in fact about 40% of the population of each. The mixture was very cosmopolitan of course with, additionally, French, Chinese, Spanish and Portuguese families. While it would not be true to say there were no colour differences, every inhabitant was first and foremost a true Trinidadian.

On the Essiquibo River – British Guiana

96

21

Assuansi. 1948

After returning to the Gold Coast as a fully-fledged Agricultural Officer, I went back to my first station, Assuansi. My duties under the Chief Agricultural Officer, also stationed at Assuansi, covered all aspects of the department in the Central Province. From Cape Coast to Assuansi, shifting cultivation and the growing of food crops had modified the former damp forest conditions, and only north of Assuansi did some degree of afforestation still provide suitable conditions for the cultivation of cocoa.

Since my initial tour the Rose's lime industry had suffered a considerable decline and the company's factories had been reduced to one. Trees in the farmers' small groves were dying right and left, but the reasons for this were obscure and not understood, and it was one of my duties to investigate the problem. While I did make exhaustive surveys of the farms, without the assistance of specialist officers I was not able to come to any direct conclusions as to the cause or causes of these outbreaks.

It was only some years later that the true nature of the disease was established. It was found that the lime trees had been killed by the Tristeza virus, which had already been responsible for the devastation of citrus in South America. No doubt this virus had been introduced in bud wood from South Africa and was then spread through the agency of aphids. While it was true that most of the lime plantations had been established as seedling trees, work was being done at Assuansi to provide superior planting material on various rootstocks, as was becoming the norm in the cultivation of citrus. It was subsequently established that the disease was lethal to limes grown on sour orange rootstocks, though it was later found that limes grown on rough lemon rootstocks proved reasonably tolerant.

Assuansi was a small station with only two or three bungalows and a rest house. Close by was a Trades school, with the proprietors of which I sometimes played mahjong of an evening. Cape Coast was of course the centre of government for the province, and provided the headquarters for all the main government departments. Together with all the representatives of the trading companies, missions, etc., the European population would have approached one hundred. There was naturally a thriving club, where it was my wont to play snooker on Saturday afternoons, and perhaps to attend on one evening a week to change the library books and socialise.

All the villages along the coastal belt were concerned with fishing. Apart from the use of hand-drawn nets along the beaches, large fishing canoes paddled out through the surf using the prevailing early morning off-the-land breeze, then returning in the late afternoons when the wind blew in from the sea. The fishing boats after reaching the shore sold their catch to the ubiquitous market mammies, who dried much of it in the sun on the beach. Many lorries carried the finished article, now appropriately referred to, at least by the Europeans, as 'stink fish', up country, even as far as the Northern Territories.

All along the coast the surf was generally heavy with fierce undertows. Except for very strong swimmers, bathing was confined to the occasional sheltered bay. A neighbour who was in the army in Accra while I was in East Africa described how a newly-arrived army officer was drowned the very first day he arrived from England. A frieze of coconut palms followed the line of most of the beaches. A feature of the coast was the old slave forts, now usually utilised as government offices or rest houses, and in the Central Province those at Elmina, Cape Coast, Apam and Senya Beraku were particularly impressive. These forts are still in a very good state of preservation, retaining their eerie dungeons and ancient cannons lining the battlements. One can easily picture the slave ships lying offshore and beyond the range of the surf. In the days of the slave trade, the coast of West Africa was a battleground between a number of European nations including the British, the Dutch, the Danes, the French and even the Swedes. Generally speaking, at that time the European traders held the coastal forts only, and relied on the chiefs from the interior to bring in the slaves and the other products that included palm oil, gold and ivory.

I have already made some comments on the subject of European/ African relationships and I would again like to make it clear that, when I refer to Europeans in perhaps a separate category to Africans, I am not talking in any racial way but am simply referring to the situation as it occurred in the 1940s. At that time Africans were being groomed for self-government, but the population as far as government officials were concerned was divided into senior and junior officers. Senior officers were allocated bungalows, and junior officers had distinctly lower accommodation. If an African officer was promoted into the senior officer category, he was treated the same as any European officer. This progression increased rapidly after the end of the war. Not so in East Africa. That was known as a country where Europeans could settle permanently and it was originally intended for Europeans to remain dominant. As will now be well known, such aspirations did not succeed, and I shall touch on this subject again later on. I had also intended here to discuss the European officer's relations with his domestic servants, but this is such an important and interesting subject that I shall devote the whole of a later chapter to this question.

Changing the subject rather abruptly, I would mention that one of the first things that strike a newcomer to West Africa is the number and variety of ants that meet him at every turn. Bungalows on agricultural stations always seemed particularly subject to the presence of ants, and lots of other insect creatures too. The brown sugar ant will rapidly invade the food if given an opportunity, and you left the top of the marmalade pot off at your peril. For this reason the legs of safes and fridges were always stood in tins of water. Don't forget to top up with a little kerosene to stop the mosquitoes breeding!

Small black ants were everywhere, and if a dead fly or other insect should fall to the ground, it was chopped up and carried away in no time. Red tailor ants were prevalent in citrus trees. They were called tailor ants as they sewed leaves together to make nests, from which they emerged quickly to attack any intruder. They had a particularly sharp bite and emitted a rather sour odour. Less unfriendly were the black tree ants which lived in mud tents stuck to the trunks.

The driver or safari ants have a ferocious reputation. They are most commonly seen when, if one is walking on bush paths, one steps over seemingly endless columns. Then they are at their most inoffensive. Occasionally such columns spread out in search of food, and then they will consume any creature in their path that is not quick enough to get out of their way. On one occasion ants invaded our kitchen at Kpeve, and were only deterred by hot ashes being spread in their path. We found a hen one morning eaten bare to the bones, but still sitting on its clutch of eggs.

Termites, or White ants as they are also known, are quite distinct from true ants. They live entirely in the dark and are very destructive to the walls of mud and wooden buildings. Even when they come out on the surface, they build themselves a roof of mud. They are quite blind. Termites are of course also found in the large cone-shaped heaps which are such a feature of the grassy plains in Africa. At the commencement of the rainy season, hordes of flying ants emerge from underground nests to be greedily devoured by birds and many other living creatures. With moths and sausage flies they bombarded the bungalow Tilley lamps, losing their wings which fell in heaps on the ground to be devoured by the resident lizards and geckos. I have never eaten these 'ants' but Africans consider them a delicacy either raw or cooked, without the wings of course. Another interesting predator usually in evidence in the bungalow or garden was the praying mantis. I never experienced problems with locusts, though large crickets were common. While walking on bush paths, one saw many large millipedes. To this day there are a number of books on my shelves exhibiting unsightly patches, or subject to internal mining of the covers. I cannot recollect what this common pest in the tropics was called, and can only describe it as a coleopterous bookworm.

It was only recently (June 1997) that I came across a very well written field guide to the Kakum National Park and the adjoining Assin Attandaso game reserve in Ghana. This locality lies only some twenty miles north of Cape Coast and not far from Assuansi. It contains most interesting lists of the animal, bird and reptile species that can be found there. It came as a great surprise to me that, when stationed at Assuansi, I was living not far away from such exciting creatures as bongo, forest elephant and both red river and giant forest hogs. The two first mentioned are stated to be relatively common. Other interesting species said to be found in the reserve are five species of duiker, bush buck, civet cats, leopard (rare), lots of monkeys, and the more usual squirrels, genets, pottos, pangolins, etc.

The explanation as to how this excellent game reserve exists without being inundated by rapacious hunters is now apparent. It occupies an area of surviving forest which from the map does not show the presence of any roads or bush villages, but a network of streams. It was created in 1989 and is 357 square kilometres in extent. Its success no doubt relies on the financial assistance of a United Nations Development programme and the United States

Agency for Industrial Development. Judging by the animal population it must be very well maintained and patrolled. It is perhaps of interest to explain here that tropical rain forests are not truly evergreen, but are actually semi-deciduous. Unlike forest in temperate regions their leaves are shed haphazardly or rotationally.

A coastal scene

22

Kumasi. 1951–52

My leave in England in 1951 was memorable for my marriage to Barbara on 1st September. Rather a whirlwind romance, I am sure, and a surprise to many people who had thought of me as a confirmed bachelor! In fact we met in June and were married in September. The wedding took place in the little church that adjoined Barbara's farmhouse at Much Fawley in Herefordshire, in a lovely position overlooking the River Wye. The best man was George Spurrell who was also in the Department of Agriculture and who owned a farm in Norfolk. He was a formidable character who had a liking for beer before breakfast.

It was not possible for Barbara to return with me on the mail ship, and she was to follow later by air. On my return I found that I had been posted to Kumasi, there to take charge of the Cocoa Agronomy Division in Ashanti. My duties were to be mainly concerned with the supervision of cocoa stations and pest and disease control work. The latter was largely aimed against the disease of Swollen Shoot, the rapid spread of which was threatening the very existence of the cocoa industry throughout the colony. I shall deal with aspects of this important work on cocoa in later chapters.

Some weeks after arriving in Kumasi I travelled down to Accra to meet Barbara at the airport after her flight, which had taken in Tripoli, Kano and Lagos. At Accra we were put up for a day or two by our Deputy Director, Alan Moss and his wife Yvonne. Then we set off for Kumasi in our heavily laden car with Kwesi, our faithful cook, and a box of day old Light Sussex chicks. The trip proved to be something of an eye-opener for Barbara as, when we reached Nkawkaw just south of the Ashanti border, heavy rains had blocked the roads, and we were obliged to spend the night at a rest house, though the local forestry officer kindly gave us dinner. The next morning a gang of Public Works Department labourers, who were at work on the road, literally carried the car and us through the floods, leaving us to travel on safely to Kumasi. When our car entered the garage of our bungalow, Barbara will not readily forget the large number of orange-headed Agama lizards that scuttled about in alarm, then curtseyed to us, as was their habit, by rapidly raising and lowering their front legs.

I have in a previous chapter given some account of life in Kumasi and Ashanti generally. Barbara took to the abundant social life in Kumasi very quickly, and also much enjoyed the travelling and staying in rest houses. There was, to me at least, one amusing incident when one afternoon Barbara was taking a siesta. She was alarmed to be woken by a gang of chanting Africans advancing on the bungalow. However, she was not about to be attacked. It was the usual gang of prisoners cutting the grass on the golf course, with the leader calling the tune with his calabash filled with pebbles. These grass cutters, incidentally, used swords made from barrel hoops and filed to a murderous sharpness. In Kumasi there was the usual surfeit of dinner parties between different bungalows, and attendance at the club was almost obligatory on Saturday nights. Indeed, there were few Sunday mornings when we did not see the light of day before returning to the bungalow for breakfast.

Of the rest houses scattered through the district, the one

overlooking Lake Bosumtwi was one of the most attractive.* Lake Bosumtwi, the only lake in the Gold Coast, is of volcanic origin and lies in a deep crater with a shoreline of some ten miles, on which there are several fishing villages. Scientifically, I believe it should be correctly termed a caldron. The steep descent to the lake's shore was almost as tiring as the severe climb out, while the hot and stuffy conditions on the shores are not hard to imagine. It is presumably a way of preserving fish stocks that the fetish of the lake allowed only primitive rafts to be used, and with no ironwork employed in their construction or in the paddles. It was rumoured that a flying boat landed on the lake during the war years, to the consternation of the inhabitants and no doubt to the spirits too. Other rest houses at which we stayed were at Bekwai, Konongo, Agogo, Berekum, Goaso, Obuasi, and in the far west at Pamu on the French border with the Ivory Coast.

In my chapter on Koforidua I have discussed the question of health at some length. When one reads old accounts about the 'White Man's Grave', the palm oil ruffians and the slave trade, the saying that the 'sun was my undoing' would seem to hold a lot of credence. In the old days it would appear that many Europeans who worked in West Africa never went home. They stayed and died. The old rhyme states:

*Roy Silverlock, an ex-Gold Coast agricultural officer, reported visiting the lake in 1992 and found that a road had been made down to the lake shore. Unaware of its appalling condition he started down it in his car, but with no chance of turning, he had to continue to the bottom. He found that the villagers no longer respected the fetish's requirements and now used conventional methods of fishing, including the use of wire-netting fish traps. There were motor launches on the lake and, of all things, evidence of water-skiing. However, all this sort of activity seemed to be in abeyance, presumably because of the condition of the approach road.

'Have you heard of the Bight of Benin,
Where few come out, but many went in?'

It is certainly true that we did not find malaria a serious threat to our health. Paludrine was certainly a wonderful drug, and perhaps there was some truth in the theory that if you drank a fair modicum of whisky, mosquitoes would leave you alone! Recent reports indicate that malarial control on the Coast has markedly deteriorated. Mosquitoes have tended to become resistant to once-successful prophylactics, while sanitary provisions are no longer so efficient. At isolated rest houses, or when addressing groups of farmers in bush villages, I was often extensively bitten by sand flies. Despite this I do not recollect being affected by sand fly fever, dengue or any of the other more obscure forest fevers.

Prickly heat was sometimes a recurring problem, particularly towards the end of a tour when one might be thought to be a little run-down. It was a well known fact that within one day of the ship leaving Freetown on leave, prickly heat would vanish. When walking in the bush, sweat bees, though they did not sting, settled in swarms on one's damp skin and clothes.

Barbara also maintained fairly good health, though she did have some mild doses of fever, and there were later certain difficulties with the children. When I first went out to the Coast, the climate was considered unsuitable for European children, particularly after the first year or two. Later on opinions were revised, and the reason why many older children were not out with their parents was due to lack of educational facilities. One thing that stuck in my mind was when Barbara discussed with an African doctor the question of her own children's feeding, he pooh-poohed the European custom of regular feeding times, saying the African mothers feed their children when they demonstrate that they are hungry. Perhaps the mammies' way of carrying the piccins on the back also avoided the necessity of getting their wind up!

Apart from malaria, there are certain other unpleasant though now comparatively rare risks that can occur in West Africa. Trypanosomiasis (sleeping sickness) is not normally contracted by Europeans, though tsetse flies are common in the forest country and so affecting the keeping of cattle and horses. They resemble the English horsefly and slyly bite in the same way. Black water and yellow fever are probably afflictions of the past, while river blindness, Bilharzia and the horrible guinea worm infection are water-borne diseases unlikely to be experienced by Europeans.

We were very dependent on the good practices of our servants to protect our food and water supplies from impurities. I have always been keen on 'living' on the country – I am not of course referring to black mammies! While of course we did buy imported food from the local Ice company, the cook concentrated on produce from the local market. Even if the eggs were small, the chickens skinny and the meat tough, I am sure we in time worked up a considerable resistance to any impurities in local produce. Towards the end of the war there were many American servicemen in the country and they imported almost 100% of their food. I would hazard an opinion that because of this they would show a very poor resistance to anything infective. Apropos of this, a young employee of Plant Protection was sent out to Bunso to coordinate their share of the cocoa disease campaign. Within only a week he died of polio. While such a fatality was most unusual, I still wonder whether an established 'Coaster' would not have shown partial if not complete resistance to such a disease.

Just a word or two about a very different subject – snakes. It surprises people to learn that, during all my years in the Gold Coast, the number of live snakes that I have seen could be numbered on the fingers of less than two hands, and this despite my having walked many hundreds of miles of bush paths during the course of my career, both through forest and savannah. Clearly, all snakes do their best to keep out of one's way, though on two occasions my car surprised black mambas about to cross the road.

The speed with which the reptiles reared up and retired back into the bush was most marked. This cobra is capable of spitting accurately into one's eye if cornered. I was always concerned about encountering another very poisonous snake, the green mamba, which, being an arboreal species, one felt might unexpectedly strike at you out of a tree. The very venomous gaboon vipers were reputedly fairly common, but though their presence was often reported to me I never saw one alive. I was on several occasions offered gaboon viper skins, and had poultry killed by them. The gaboon viper can grow to over five feet in length and be as thick as one's calf. In more open country are found two more big vipers – the puff adder and the horned cerastes, or rhinoceros viper.

During our Sojourn on the Coast, Africans often brought us odd animals and birds to adopt as pets. Monkeys and African Grey Parrots were the commonest, though at Jasikan in Togoland we were once offered for purchase a baby crocodile in a bucket. Our sole acquisition however was the Maxwell's Duiker referred to later.

23

Kpeve. 1949–50 and 1954

After the First World War, the German West African colonies of Togoland and the Cameroons were taken over by the Allies and attached to their neighbouring British and French territories. The Gold Coast acquired a long and narrow strip of Togoland, never much more than 30 to 40 miles wide and running from the Northern Territories down to a point near the French port of Lomé. As far as the Agricultural Department was concerned, the administrative district of Trans Volta/Togoland also included a portion of the colony to the east of the Volta river and running from Senchi ferry, south of Akuse down to the lower Volta ferry at Ada. This area included an important piece of land on the coast between Ada and Lomé, only a few miles wide with the large Keta lagoon to its north.

The agricultural district of Trans Volta/Togoland had its headquarters at Kpeve (the K not pronounced) which was some 20 miles away from the administrative centre of Ho. Kpeve was always my favourite Gold Coast station, and I had two tours there in 1949–50 and 1954. Why did I like Kpeve? Perhaps because it was so remote and one felt that one was really living in tropical Africa and master of all one surveyed. When I was there in 1950 the telephone was laid on. While this was to the delight of the local villagers, who celebrated with libations of palm wine, to me

The Bungalow, Kpeve

the direct telephonic communication with Head Office in Accra lost to some extent Kpeve's feeling of living in the bush.

As Agricultural officer in charge of Trans Volta/Togoland, I had a nice bungalow with a pretty garden and a commanding view over the station and the surrounding plains and hills. There was also a rest house and what was known as the German Bungalow, which of course dated back to German times. It is a wonder how its thick mud walls had stood up so well against the continual attacks of termites. At the time I was in Kpeve, this bungalow was usually in the occupation of the survey officer in charge of cocoa industry affairs. The station grew the usual farm crops and some cocoa and coffee. There was a flock of sheep, and some cattle which were used for ploughing, though a Ferguson tractor appeared later.

The Provincial Commissioner was stationed at Ho, where there was the usual range of bungalows for senior government officials. The only other important centre in Togoland was Hohoe (pronounced Hofwe) some 35 miles north of Kpeve, which was an important trading centre. Otherwise, there were only District Commissioners at Kpandu and Jasikan. Numerous schools and missions of several denominations were spread about, and one or two senior customs officers patrolled the borders with the French territory.

A feature of Togoland was the incredibly rough roads. These were of laterite composition and were either severely pot-holed in the rainy season or badly corrugated in dry weather. Then the big 'mammy' lorries moved in clouds of dust, marking their approach for miles. The road from Golokwati to Hohoe was particularly noted for its very large corrugations. I am not sure why roads developed such surfaces. If one drove a car at a slow speed, the going was very rough, though if one speeded up to forty miles an hour, a comparatively smooth ride could be attained. Broken springs were frequent expendable items.

In my first tour at Kpeve I possessed a Morris Oxford car

which, needless to say, was quite unsuitable for roads of this nature. When on trek near Keta, the steering packed up without warning, depositing the car into the bush. I escaped injury, though the agricultural overseer with me had some facial cuts. I then purchased a Standard Vanguard saloon which proved marginally more robust. American cars and pickups were of course more suitable for the existing conditions. A problem with driving in the Gold Coast was the necessity of avoiding straying livestock, particularly sheep, goats and chickens in the villages. Despite taking the utmost care, however, few trips were completed without at least one casualty.

Much of the Togoland landscape was featureless orchard bush, i.e. typical 'Mamoba' country. Most of the cocoa was grown in the more forested country north of Jasikan, or where rivers and streams provided some gallery foresting which produced moister conditions and some shade.

The Keta district was visited on trek at least once a month. South of Ho, grassland conditions became dominant, and there were stands of borassus palm and many of the strange-looking baobabs. These bulbous elephantine trees did not grow very high, but had enormous girth and were reputed to grow to a great age. Another feature of this district was the presence of many isolated inselbergs, smaller editions of the kopjes of South Africa. I always wanted to explore one but never did. When I reached the Keta littoral I usually stayed at rest houses at Denu or at Keta itself. A feature of cash crops along the coast was a thriving shallot industry. These shallots were grown very intensively using underground sources of water and were exported from here all over the colony. Coconuts were another important crop and were also exported, both in the form of fresh nuts or as copra. A disease of coconuts was widespread. It was known at Cape St Paul's wilt, and was carried by the large rhinoceros beetles that are found on the palms. Pigs were kept in large numbers running among the houses and under the palms. I did not encourage my cook to purchase pork from this source, however, for fairly obvious reasons of sanitation!

If one travelled to Keta from Accra, it was necessary to cross the Volta at Sogonkope using the lower Volta ferry. The river was about half a mile wide at this point, and the ferry, capable of carrying some half a dozen lorries or cars, was lashed to a powerful launch. I stayed at the rest house at Sogonkope on several occasions, and was once marooned there when heavy rains made the roads impassable. As a result I had to abandon the car and escape up the river to Akuse, where I could be picked up from Kpeve.

Denu was only a mile or two from the frontier and the French town of Lomé. There it was pleasant to visit the Hotel de Golfe and sample the cuisine with the numerous French residents. Also from Ho we occasionally crossed over into French country to visit the town of Palime, usually returning with supplies of wine and brandy. A spectacular waterfall near Palime was a popular venue for picnics, and provided good footage for my ciné camera.

On one memorable occasion we were invited to lunch by the French manager of a palm oil factory close to Palime. Arriving about midday, we were a little bit disappointed to be offered only one bottle of beer before going in to lunch. I should explain that it was the habit of British residents in West Africa to have a number of drinks before a late lunch! However, on this occasion, little did we know that the lunch would last several hours and consist of five or six courses with a different wine with each! It was quite clear that much of the food had been imported from France. Naturally a good time was had by all.

Barbara was with me for my second tour at Kpeve and she also liked Kpeve. She became used to accompanying me on trek and staying in rest houses. These rest houses were usually of a rather primitive nature and sparsely furnished, though it was no longer necessary to carry with us camp beds, baths, etc. Despite this, camp beds would have been an improvement over certain notorious rest house mattresses. As most rest houses had open verandas, to Barbara's consternation bats were always hawking in and out, though they were of course reducing the mosquito population. Lavatories equipped with the usual 'thunder boxes' were small rooms at the rear, where there was always the risk of a lurking mamba! Rest house bookings had to be made in advance through the local DC. All rest houses had a visitors' book, and it was interesting to read the comments, often humorous, of previous residents. An old Blackwoods magazine invariably seemed to be present among the reading matter.

Sometimes Barbara stayed behind while I was away. It says a lot for the trustworthiness of the West African servants that I could leave her alone in a bungalow in the middle of the bush in the sole charge of the cook or steward boy. At Kpeve the garden boy, Hassan, was detailed to sleep outside her bedroom as 'watchnite'. Perhaps even she was a little bit perturbed when he complained one morning of spirits troubling him in the night. At Kpeve drumming from neighbouring villages would often continue for much of the night. The boys would ascribe this to 'tigare' – juju palaver.

Social life in Togoland was somewhat limited by the distances involved, but parties flared up from time to time. However, every evening we sat on the stoep contemplating Africa, with the steward boy passing drinks as required. In the dry season the distant hills would be ringed with bushfires. Moon flowers grew on the front wall of the veranda with their blossoms appearing at night time only. There was also a pretty climber growing on the walls – *petrea volubilis*. Our daughter Petrea was named after this plant. At a speech at her wedding many years later, the 'volubilis' part of her name caused considerable amusement!

Before my arrival in Togoland, four residents – Deryk Westwood, Agriculture; Dizzie Dennis, DC Kpandu; Banochie, the Education Officer from Ho; and the Customs Officer, whose name I have forgotten – had formed a convivial alliance and met frequently. From them I learnt about 'Sidi Barrani'. If one's glass was unfortunately empty, you announced to the company, 'Have

Farewell party, Kpeve

you ever been in Sidi Barrani?' While this predicament didn't happen very often, the host would always take immediate action. Since leaving the Coast I have used this ploy in England from time to time but with mixed success. I was pleased to come across Banochie at a later date at the Andromeda Gardens in Barbados.

To mention one rather amusing incident. A rather pompous Agricultural Survey Officer named George Baxter was living in the German bungalow. One ordinary weekday he asked me round to lunch. This was before my wife came out, so there were only the two of us. Imagine my surprise when he had an argument with his steward boy for setting my plate on his left side rather than on his right! Between two people on an extremely bush station this seemed to be carrying etiquette a bit too far – indeed a bit Somerset Maugham-ish. Baxter's wife, a very pleasant Danish lady called Elinor, came out later. She organised a really splendid smorgasbord party with many separate dishes which took several days to prepare. During the meal we tossed down numerous small glasses of

115

aquavit followed by the usual pints of cold lager beer as chasers.

In the dry season (December to April in particular) it really was very hot at Kpeve, and the temperature was probably in excess of 90°F at midday. Generally speaking I would close the office at one or two p.m. and retire to the bungalow for lunch and a siesta. The office messenger Ben, who was also a useful barber, would bring up any letters that required signature. To illustrate how hot it really was, a pig was killed for a barbecue the following day, for an agricultural show, I think. By night time it was smelling and had to be thrown out. A sheep was slaughtered instead at the last moment.

While at Kpeve we adopted a young Maxwells duiker. This proved easy to tame and a delightful pet, running in and out of the bungalow at will. Only after some time did we find that the duiker always relieved itself in the same corner of the lounge, with a rotting effect on the carpet at that point. I have since read that duikers were known to be difficult to housetrain!

Just a few more accounts about rest houses. We liked staying at a rest house at a village called Amedjofe although it was only about 30 miles from Kpeve. It was popular as it had an altitude of over 2,500 feet, and it was feasible for the rest house keeper to light a fire for the occupant in the evening. Like the one at Mpraeso it also smoked badly! Another rest house was at Anum, and I once visited it from Accra. While it had spectacular views over the Volta river some distance below, it was in a very remote district and had the reputation of being haunted. The cook walked down to the river and returned several hours later with some excellent fish. West African cooks were certainly not lazy and would go to a lot of trouble to please their 'strange' European employers. What I remember most about the visit, however, was that in the night the bed collapsed! It was not easy to extricate oneself in the pitch darkness in this supposedly haunted building, and the steward boy out of call!

24

Accra. 1953 and 1956

In addition to my few weeks in Head Office in 1939, I had two further spells in Accra on relieving duties. Living in Accra had many advantages. Bungalows were better equipped and more up-to-date and there were excellent shopping facilities. The Kingsway Stores and the Ice Company were indeed the forerunners of today's supermarkets, and there was even a newly-opened luxury hotel – the Ambassador. On the other hand, one found oneself largely confined to the fixed hours of an office environment.

Accra was of course headquarters of the Governor of the colony, whose residence was at Christiansborg Castle, a white battlemented structure seemingly rising straight out of the foaming surf. Here, as elsewhere along the coast, huge seas raced and thrashed against the African shelf. The castle had been magnificently restored after its early days of the slave trade, and contained a maze of corridors, inner courtyards and well-kept gardens. The Danes were said to be the original builders as long ago as 1659, and then followed occupation by several other European nations, Great Britain finally taking over.

In the old days, and before the advent of anti-malarial drugs, West Africa was, as far as Europeans were concerned, a very unhealthy country, and indeed it was rumoured that no Dutch or Danish Governor returned home alive throughout a period of 140 years! My experience of the castle amounted to my signing, as a civil servant, the Governor's book at the gates and being once invited there to a cocktail party. Latterly the castle became the residence of the President of the new African state – Kwami Nkrumah.

Apart from the ever-present roar of the surf there was also an ever-present daytime noise – the continuous chorus of car horns emanating from the town, and particularly from the busy Station Road. Africans always made full use of their car horns. The European Club was the largest in the colony and provided restaurant facilities and some rest house accommodation. When I first arrived in West Africa, it was true that such clubs were strictly European only. Later on Africans were encouraged to join, though in actual fact few did.

The cook had abundant supplies of fresh produce available in Accra market, making the purchase of any of the wide range of

Christiansborg Castle, Accra

118

imported products virtually an extravagance. All varieties of local fish were available, and sometimes turtle meat for as little as 1/- a pound. In the larger markets such as those at Accra and Kumasi, a bewildering range of commodities was always available for purchase. Apart from all manner of foods, fresh, dried and tinned, there would be bush meat, cane rats, trussed-up fowls and live sheep and goats. Also cotton good, metal ware, kerosene and kerosene lamps, patent medicines and lots of small articles such as candles, mammy powder, combs, etc., etc.

There would be both men and women operating sewing machines and, if you were illiterate, there would be letter-writers to carry out your correspondence. There were bars selling palm wine, and perhaps the more formidable but illegal 'apateshi', and mammies selling stews redolent of dried fish and red hot pepper. The bread on sale was normally 'sugar' bread, not appreciated by Europeans, though our cooks were capable of making excellent bread as we were used to. There were of course stalls selling all sorts of peculiar native medicines, and where parts of monkeys, lizards and birds were in evidence there was no doubt a juju connection.

The large markets were normally ruled by influential market mammies who had always monopolised most of the trade in the country, or at least in African circles. The activities of these mammies ranged from the few powerful ones, who bought enormous quantities from the wholesalers, to small girls walking the street and selling as little as a single cigarette or three or four lumps of sugar. While the rich mammies might handle goods worth thousands of pounds, they tended to carry transaction details in their heads, and while some might use banks, they would often carry large sums of money concealed within their voluminous native clothes. The bush markets are more produce-orientated, and opening confined to one or two days in the week.

Markets are of course the meeting place of the 'mammy wagons', which carry mixed loads of passengers and goods all over the country. These vehicles were imported into the country only as chassis, after which the seats and canopies were constructed locally. It was noteworthy that the front seats were not provided with doors, perhaps allowing the driver to escape quickly if an accident seemed imminent! Anyway, drivers were seldom killed or injured. These lorries were usually filled to the brim with passengers accompanied with their loads of foodstuffs and perhaps even livestock. When one's car passes lorries from the coast carrying fish, the prevailing odour accompanies one for some time afterwards, though no doubt the passengers in such lorries become inured to the smell. I am reliably informed that nowadays much of the traffic is carried by minibuses which may be flagged down anywhere and at any time. They are apparently called tro-tros.

While many of the lorries were in bad condition, none was considered roadworthy without a newly-painted slogan both on the back and front. The variety and humour of these captions is well known. The subjects are legion and I can only give a few examples here. Fairly common ones are 'Let them say', 'No time to die' and 'Be content with your lot'. Religious subjects include 'The lord is my Shepherd and 'God knows why'. More cynical drivers have slogans on the lines of, 'Money rules All', 'Poor no Friend, and 'Fear Women'. An honest slogan is 'Money is the root of all joy'. Everyone in Ghana has a favourite. Mine is the wonderfully ambiguous 'GO LIKE HELL AND YOU WILL GET THERE'

So far I have made no mention of currency. When I was on the Coast, it was still pounds, shillings and pence, though smaller coins right down to a tenth of a penny had holes through the middle like washers. This type of coinage was often rather rudely referred to as 'monkey money'. Nowadays of course, the pound has become the cedi. As late as the twenties and thirties cowry shells as collected from the beaches were still used as a form of money in primitive parts of West Africa. Europeans liked to collect

120

these shells and also the tenth-of-a-penny coins to use as counters for card games.

Roy Silverlock paints a very different picture of modern day Accra. It must now be a city of about a million inhabitants with its perimeters extended by miles and particularly towards the Aburi scarp. On the outskirts are many new housing estates while the poorer and slummier parts of Accra are now even more over-crowded with people coming into town from the bush to look for work. The big stores have largely been split up but there are a number of small supermarkets and the Syrian and Indian traders are still a dominant force.

The streets are clogged with traffic, buses run regularly and there are many itinerant taxis. The main streets are also lined with petty traders all trying to make a living. There are now a number of restaurants and hotels ranging in size and importance up to the five star Labadi Beach Hotel. There are many bars and some swinging night clubs which Europeans can visit safely and unescorted. In fact the people appear to remain just as friendly as they used to be.

I have recently acquired some tapes of present day Ghanaian music. I found these very well produced with an attractive beat, the singing in the vernacular and not in English. They are more sophisticated than the old style high life, and the sound is quite different from music from the Caribbean or Western World Jazz.

25

Bunso. 1953, 1955–58

Our last two tours, apart from a short spell in Accra, were spent at Bunso and they were very enjoyable ones. Bunso, the main cocoa station for the colony, was some 1,736 acres in extent, and sited in a rural area in the eastern region, 20 miles north of Koforidua and only ten miles from the West African Cocoa Research Station at Tafo. My work during these years was mainly concerned with cocoa, and I will be devoting further chapters to discussing this in more detail.

Meanwhile, about our life at Bunso.* The bungalow again was a most attractive one. It was situated some two miles from the main station and was approached by a winding road bordered by impressive royal palms and lined with many species of ferns and, in places, gigantic creepers. The bungalow was set on a low hilltop and among an arboretum of forest trees. It was quite isolated from the main station, the offices of which, and some ten or more bungalows, were visible from the bungalow's stoep, with further glimpses of the forest beyond and ranges of distant hills.

Around the bungalow were many flowering trees – pink cassias,

*Bunso bungalow. Not long after my retirement, my successor at Bunso lost the occupancy of this delightful bungalow. It was taken over by the African Regional Commissioner at Koforidua as a weekend amenity. In actual fact I believe it was little used, and its maintenance deteriorated.

bauhinias, frangipani, a bottle brush and a fine tulip tree. There were all the usual shrubs and climbers – hibiscus, bougainvillia, alamanda, plumbago, morning glory, coralyta, etc., with banks of cannas, anthurium lilies, cleodendrons (pagoda flowers) and of course the usual zinnias and marigolds found in all African gardens. Verbena and other flowers draped the low walls. Many people in West Africa endeavoured to grow English roses. While they would grow reasonably well, lacking dormancy they tended to flower all the year round, and consequently the blooms were small.

Our Light Sussex hens and Muscovy ducks wandered about the lawns. As a novelty we had imported a donkey named Pepe from the Northern Territories, which was kept tethered near the bungalow and in the charge of the garden boy, Yamba, who, being from the Northern Territories himself, was well used to handling donkeys. Pepe did not take too kindly to being ridden by our many visitors, and I do remember it being assisted up the steps

Bungalow, Bunso

123

into the bungalow itself during a party we had one Christmas! The tame duiker we had brought over from Togoland unfortunately disappeared when we were absent on leave. Possibly one of the locals could not resist the chance of such tempting 'bush meat'.

The bungalow had one rather alarming aspect – its position on highish ground seemed to attract the violent electrical storms that are a feature of the forest regions in the rainy season. On those occasions blue flashes appeared to play around the bungalow, but fortunately nothing serious happened during our occupancy. These storms normally occurred in the early evenings, and though the rain was torrential, they rarely persisted more than an hour or two. Occasionally, however, as much as five or six inches would fall in one night. Rainfall at Bunso would have been in the region of 60 inches a year. In the rainy season one was often awakened during the night by the noise of large trees in the surrounding forest crashing down. Their roots had been weakened by the rain-softened ground.

At Bunso, as with other bungalows we stayed in, when we were perhaps having a rest in the afternoon, the galvanised tin roof would give out loud noises like gunshots as the roof expanded in the sun, later to cool in the late afternoon. While the bungalow with its verandas and double quarters was fully mosquito proofed, the department regularly sprayed around all bungalows using motorised knapsack sprayers and DDT. The use of DDT for such a purpose nowadays would of course be frowned upon. This reminds me of the maize from the farm with which we fed our poultry. This grain, after having been treated to excess with gamma BHC against weevils, caused the fowls' eggs and even the poultry meat to develop a distinctly fusty taste!

Jonathan, our eldest son, then in his twos and threes, gave us one or two frights. Members of the Cadbury family used to make annual visits to the country to assess the cocoa prospects. On one occasion when I was showing Mr and Mrs Cadbury round the plantation, a message came through announcing that Jonathan had cut his nose badly on a watering can, and his mother had had to take him off to hospital nearly 20 miles away instead of supervising the preparation of lunch. I am quite sure the servants coped satisfactorily, however.

On another occasion, approaching dusk, and this period in the tropics was always short, Jonathan was nowhere to be found. After a frantic search, it could only be concluded that he had strayed into and got lost in the surrounding forest. Taking the car, I rushed off down to the station to raise a search party. On the main road, however, I encountered a herd of Zebu cattle, the herders of which were taking no notice of the unusual sight of a very small white boy walking along the road in the opposite direction, bound for who-knows-where. One can imagine the relief when I returned him to his mother!

Entertaining was always an important feature of life in the tropics, particularly when one's seniority increased. Visitors of varying degrees of importance visited Bunso, and it was up to the head of the station to entertain them – without any entertainment allowance, I might add. Apart from this, there was a great deal of socialising between the local residents, including 'country chop' lunches which I will be describing. Frequent visits were made to the clubs at Tafo and Koforidua to play snooker, change library books and sometimes to attend dances and other functions. There were of course no drink/driving regulations on the Coast in those days. One drove to and fro from parties with no thought of how much alcohol had been consumed. While it is true that the volume of traffic was much less than occurs nowadays, I have no recollection of any drink/driving problems concerning Europeans. I am sure that this was partly due to the fact that the Europeans concerned were of a more mature age, and more responsible than the young people that now drive in this country.

A much bigger problem to me was the necessity of keeping awake when driving in the heat of the day. On one occasion I did have a very narrow escape. Driving on trek one day with the

Royal Palm Avenue, Bunso

family all asleep in the car, and having been up late the night before, I dozed off myself, only to be woken by the blaring of a horn. Just in time I avoided a full-frontal collision with a very large mammy lorry. If he had not used his horn to such good effect, it is doubtful if any of us would be here today to tell the tale.

With the bungalow at Bunso being in such an isolated position, I did manage to get the telephone installed during my tenure of office. We were, however, still dependent on Tilley lamps, and bath water was still heated on the kitchen fire and carried to the bath by kerosene tin. We of course possessed a large kerosene refrigerator and received regular weekly deliveries of cold foods from the Ice Company in Accra.

All the local fruits were grown on the station – citrus, mangos, guavas, pawpaws, pineapples and bananas. A variety of bread fruit, the breadnut tree, provided a very acceptable chestnut-like side-dish for 'smallchop' with the evening drinks. Regarding oranges and other citrus fruits, it is not always realised that in the tropics they have green skins. Maize cobs were always a popular addition to the menu, and the cook made a lot of use of the leaves of the cocoyam (native term – Kuntumeli) as a substitute for spinach. The garden boy usually cultivated a small garden of European vegetables which grew with mixed success. European potatoes did not do well in the Gold Coast, and could only be raised rather poorly at some higher altitudes. However, other roots such as yams and sweet potatoes could be used as substitutes. One commodity that was definitely not available was fresh milk. We got used to tinned milk, however, in our tea. A great delicacy was palm cabbage, but an extravagance, as its use involved the felling of the whole oil palm.

The time has now come to talk about 'Country Chops', i.e. groundnut stews, palm oil stews or West African curries. Our bungalow at Bunso was a lovely place to hold such feasts, but I am referring to meals that were taken at weekends in most

European bungalows throughout the colony. We normally indulged in such repasts on Sundays, though sometimes on Saturdays as well. After breakfast, the cook was given instructions as to what the meal was to be and how many guests were to be expected. After setting his wife or mammy to commence pounding the groundnuts or palm nuts, he went off to market to purchase the necessary small vegetables, eggs and chickens for the meal. Chickens or other meats were not hung and were used at once before rigor mortis set in.

To most 'Coasters' a country chop was an enjoyable experience. There would be plenty of rice or, if one wished to be more African, there would be fufu in addition. Fufu is a farinaceous food based on yam, cassava or plantain pounded into a glutinous white preparation in a wooden pot – it was not rolled under mammies' armpits as the rumour went! The ultimate test of fufu was to toss it up to the ceiling. If it stuck there it was of good consistency. West African stews and curries were much soupier than their Indian counterparts. The soup always contained vegetables such as tomatoes, onions, garden eggs and okra (often referred to as ladies' fingers) and of course plenty of red hot chilli peppers. Then came the side dishes, sometimes as many as twenty. These would include tomatoes, onions and bananas, all both fresh and fried, ginger, coconut, groundnut, grapefruit, orange, pineapple, dried fish, etc., and of course more peppers. Incidentally, among the many varieties of African peppers, some small green ones were the hottest of all and, looking innocuous, they could be a dangerous pitfall. After several helpings of the main course, accompanied of course with wine, the follow-up was inevitably fresh fruit salad, usually referred to as Jungle Juice. Knives and forks are not used when eating groundnut stews – always fork and spoon.

I omitted to mention that the stew should always contain hard boiled eggs, one for each diner. Woe betide the diner who took two! I recollect an old cartoon in Punch entitled, 'Who took the agent's egg?' – the agent, of course, was the District Commissioner.

If one took meals with Africans, we would normally have a pepper soup, usually a meal with fufu rather than rice, very hot in peppers and without the side dishes. I remember being invited to a meal with an African magistrate in Koforidua when the meal of roast turkey was unexpectedly followed by a groundnut stew. I think this was a measure to impress the Europeans rather than to typify African food.

Before the meal was served, considerable time was given up to conversation and drinking – large bottles of cold lager to start with, then pink gin. In those days, when most people smoked, a tin of fifty cigarettes was at each guest's table. There were not many teetotallers then, but if you were one at a country chop it could be quite a tedious experience, as the meal was seldom served before three or four o'clock in the afternoon, and sometimes much later. The old Coaster found it difficult to switch from the delights of the gin and bitters and scintillating conversation to the equal delights of the table. One well-known host would at intervals tell his steward boy Kofi, 'Tell cook pass chop ten minutes.' The cook well knew that this was an order not to be obeyed for the meantime. I believe that this is not a sentiment confined to the west coast of Africa. I myself have sympathy with Kingsley Amis whose dreaded phrase was, 'I think we will go straight into dinner.'

While on leave or after retirement it is a temptation to have a groundnut stew at home in England. While it is feasible with the use of peanut butter to provide a reasonable groundnut, it never seems quite right under temperate conditions. We now prefer to make a more lookalike West African curry.

Finally, a few paragraphs about birds. I have already mentioned bulbuls, the Senegal coucal and nightjars. With regard to predators, everywhere in the Gold Coast you will see vultures hopefully waiting for something to turn up. Kites and small hawks are always in evidence and like to attend bush fires to catch the insects and small rodents escaping. In the forest, fish eagles resembling the European ospreys are often seen. The commonest hornbill is the Allied, with its dipping flight and characteristic call. The black and white crows are the chief representatives of the Corvidae. Apart from the pied kingfisher so common on the river Volta, the other kingfishers are more brightly coloured and are often found in the forest and farms and far away from water. Pigeons and doves are everywhere, and in grassland areas the white egrets may be seen riding on the backs of the cattle.

Of the smaller species, colonies of weaver birds may be found close to human habitations. The sunbirds are brilliant little birds whose long thin beaks enable them to feed on the honey of garden and forest flowers. They are the counterparts of the American hummingbirds.* Sometimes one sees a male whydah with its incredibly long breeding season tail. Commonly seen on roadside telegraph wires would be the smart black and white fiscal shrikes. There is no space here to mention all the other birds including the owls, swallows and swifts, plantain eaters, parrots, bee eaters, woodpeckers and cuckoos.

Just before Christmas 1953 I took Barbara down to Accra for the arrival of our firstborn. After a short stay in the club rest house, she was admitted to the Ridge Hospital for Jonathan to be born on December 21st, almost a Christmas baby. I well remember visiting the hospital on Christmas morning for a lunch party provided by the nurses. The matron asked me to help distribute the drinks. She couldn't have chosen a more suitable person! It was not long after this that we transferred from Bunso to Togoland. On the way we stopped at the rest house at Senchi ferry to feed the baby. We were soon surrounded by admiring mammies who had probably not seen a white baby before.

This reminds me of another occasion when we ourselves were stationed in Accra, and Margot Westwood, a good friend of ours,

---

*Hummingbirds are not found in West Africa but are confined to America and the West Indies. I was intrigued to see a hummingbirds' nest and eggs in a cocoa plantation in Trinidad. It was a neat little thing though no larger than a half a crown in size.

was staying with us, for a similar reason. This was a much more protracted episode, somewhat frustrating for Margot and possibly for Barbara as well! In those days, smoking and drinking were not considered particularly undesirable in pregnancy, and I recollect Margot saying that all she wanted for breakfast was pot of tea and a packet of cigarettes!

I will now jump forward a bit. Petrea, our second child, was born in England on 1st November 1956, when Barbara was staying with her sister in Hampshire and I had returned to Ghana after leave. When I went down to Takoradi to meet Barbara with Jonathan and the new baby, I learnt that they had had a very rough passage, and gathered that they had hardly left the cabin for the first week. Baby Petrea had certainly not suffered any ill effects, however, and presented a picture of roly-poly good health.

Readers will have noticed that when proceeding to or from leave, I or my family would normally travel by sea and not by air. This was because my contract stipulated that I should be allowed sea transport, indeed a privilege not to be lost, as two weeks' sea travel on each voyage represented two weeks' extra leave. After I had left West Africa, Elder Dempster Lines must have had increasing difficulty in filling the passenger space on their two mail ships, the *Accra* and the *Appapa*. The Europeans still working on the Coast would then have been constrained to travel by air, and this no doubt accounted for the subsequent demise of the Elder Dempster company in West Africa. It is indeed a little surprising that the two ships lasted as long as 1967 and 1968 respectively. The diminution of the sea trade with West Africa must also have had a depressing effect on the prosperity of the port of Liverpool.

26

Servants

Servants played such an important part in the life of expatriates in West Africa that I will devote a separate chapter to them. Servants in the Gold Coast came from many backgrounds. They might be Accra boys, Ashantis, natives of the Northern Territories, Kru boys from Liberia, Nigerians, etc. With 'pidgin' their lingua franca they, on the whole, got on pretty well together. If additions were made to the staff list, however, it usually turned out that the newcomer came from the same tribe. In fact the 'old boy' network was very much alive on the Coast! A newcomer might wonder why so many of the boys had similar names, e.g. Kofi, Kwami, Kodjo and Kwesi. This was because these were the days in the week, and most Gold Coast boys were named according to the day of the week when they were born – girls, of course, similarly.*

Day		Male Names	Female Names
KWASIDA	(Sunday)	KWASI	AKOSUA
DWODA	(Monday)	KWADWO	ADWOWA
BENADO	(Tuesday)	KWABENA	ABENAA
WUKUDA	(Wednesday)	KWAKU	AKUA
YAWDA	(Thursday)	KWAW (YAW)	YAA
FIDA	(Friday)	KOFI	AFUA
MEMENEDA	(Saturday)	KWAME	AMMA

These names are used by members of the Twi and Fante tribes in the South of Ghana and Ashanti. Boys and girls from the Northern territories have a different range of names.

Chippo (Cook), Yamba (Garden Boy) and Patti (Steward Boy) with Jonathan

While a bachelor might content himself with a cook/steward, a married couple would normally require both a cook and a steward. Only large establishments would justify a second steward, but many households would be prevailed upon to take on a small boy, though he might be considered as much a fag for the other domestic staff as a helper in the house. In the 1940s remuneration for a cook or steward would be in the region of £4 to £6 a month, with a small boy as little as 10/- a month. Some households also employed a garden boy, a driver and a watchman. Nursemaids were sometimes employed by families, though the male servants always seemed to love children and were prepared to look after them at any time.

In West Africa all conversation with the servants and between themselves was conducted in 'pidgin' English, though on no account would you have addressed literate Africans in this way. There is no room to discuss 'pidgin' here in any depth, but a few examples are: 'Make you go' for go, 'one time' instead of at once, 'Go look proper' instead of go and see carefully 'Pass chop, drinks, meals' etc. instead of serve. Food was always 'Chop'! A tip was a 'dash', 'piccin' for child, 'Hulla Hulla' for noisy argument. Speaking of one of my friends who had a lively reputation, my cook remarked to me, 'that massa, he make night for day'!

Servants, with their varying characters and attainments, were always a subject of interest and a big talking point with their expatriate employers. Qualified servants were issued with licences, with space for all employers to record their comments at the end of a work period. Like entries in rest house books these remarks always made intriguing reading. While most comments were reasonably complimentary, one had to be prepared to read between the lines. For instance the popular sobriquet 'a good plain cook' might be an entry to be viewed with some suspicion! Very dubious comments were seldom entered in the licence, and if they were, they would have been a little hard to live down as the books appeared to last many years. Cooks who had worked for high-powered senior government officials' wives would, in particular, be very proud of glowing attributes to their culinary skills.

Servants' quarters would be considered pretty austere by modern day standards, but in those days at least they appeared to be considered quite acceptable. They were usually small concrete cells, unfurnished, and situated at the rear of the bungalow. The nearby kitchen would be of similar construction, and containing little more than a wood-burning 'Dover' stove. The cook would garner the firewood from the nearby bush, or, if in a town like Accra, it would have to be purchased in the market. Bachelors would probably never inspect their kitchens, and wives, if and when they did, were often startled by the large fly population. No ill effects seemed to occur, however,

It was considered quite acceptable to summon servants by shouting for them, though the use of their names would latterly have been considered preferable to just shouting, 'boy!' I did at

Bunso install a bell system attached to my chair, with one ring for the steward and two for the cook. People would always be asking what would three rings be for? I usually replied, 'the dancing girls!' If one of the servants was absent when called, the invariable reply would be, 'He go latrine, Sah.' It might be thought that with the servants' wages such a small proportion of their master's, they might be inclined to help themselves to food or, for that matter, from the bottles on the sideboard. My experience was that this seldom happened. The servants preferred their own foods cooked by their wives or mammies and, in the case of drinks, their own palm wine.

With regard to the latter question, this brings to mind a cook we employed at Bunso whose licence mentioned that he was a skilled pastry cook. I had returned from the office in the late afternoon and was sitting on the stoep reading reports. The cook approached. 'Massa, what would you like for breakfast?' Rather puzzled by the time of day, I replied, 'It's a little early, cook, but I will have scrambled eggs.' To my surprise, the cook shortly appeared with breakfast! Afterwards, I realised he had been on the palm wine or something stronger, and having woken up, thought it was morning! Cooks were often addressed as 'Cuckoo'. This was a complimentary term and not a derisory one. I have already mentioned how servants would borrow additional tableware etc. from neighbouring bungalows, or exchange warm beer for cold when supplies of the latter had run out. These transactions would usually be carried out by the boys themselves, and with their masters knowing nothing about it.

Cooks were seldom put out. If one for instance announced at short notice that several extra people were coming to dinner, they would not bat an eyelid. Some extra water would no doubt be added to the soup, and a few extra ingredients included in the main course. At lunch time a fowl wandering about in front of us would suddenly disappear and appear again roasted on the table in an hour or two! Cooks also had the knack of keeping meals acceptable and hot, however late the master returned from the club or elsewhere. The well-accepted opinion of the English housewife that, unless absolute punctuality was maintained, meals can be completely spoilt, is to me at least a belief that does not hold water.

It was a routine every morning that the cook should appear before his master or mistress to decide on the day's menus, and to record his purchases in the market the day before. A daily visit to the market was of course essential, some of the main requirements being bones for soup, chickens or meat, eggs, fruit and such small vegetables as onions and tomatoes. Stores were available in the bungalows to keep a range of tinned foods etc. as visits to the shops might only be possible weekly, or perhaps much less frequently. Whether such stores were kept locked was a varying feature between different employers.

Steward boys were provided with smart white uniforms and cummerbunds, particularly when serving meals or drinks, though bare feet were the rule in the bungalow. The steward boy was responsible for keeping the bungalow spotlessly clean, and being available at all times of the day to answer his master's call. While it is true the hours were long, the steward's work was not particularly onerous.

Night watchmen, or as they were more usually termed 'watchnites' were often considered necessary, particularly after the war, though it was fairly clearly accepted that they spent the greater part of their time asleep. Jokes were sometimes played on watchnites found asleep when their masters returned to the bungalow after a night out. I recall on one occasion putting a dried puff adder skin next to the sleeper to greet him when he woke up. Unfortunately he woke up unexpectedly, and threatened me with his spear! To be fair, at Kumasi the 'watchnite' Awuni, did walk around the bungalow quite a lot. To my frequent cry of, 'All correct, Awuni?' would come the response, 'All correct, Sah.'

Washing of clothes was done either by the employer's steward boy or by a communal washerman. Standards were high, though large quantities of Reckitt's starch and Robin's Blue were used. I was surprised to observe at Kpeve the washerman skilfully spraying water from his mouth to dampen the clothes he was ironing. He thought this quite a normal thing to do! Large charcoal irons were used, and quite a lot of charcoal was necessary. On no account were the clothes to be dried on the ground, which risked the wearer having later on to have 'jiggers' removed from his toes or elsewhere.

Most Europeans thought a lot of their servants, and many paid them retainers when they were on leave and continued to send them 'dashes' long after they had left the Coast. The servants never seemed to mind working long or perhaps unsociable hours. They probably took pride in the scale of their employers' entertaining, and in any case, there would be other weekends when their masters would be dining at somebody else's bungalow.

Septic tank lavatories were confined to large centres such as Accra and Kumasi. 'Small rooms' in bungalows were equipped with 'thunder boxes' which could be emptied from the outside in the early mornings. The grating of the metal container being withdrawn at that time was a familiar noise and was carried out by the 'Tankass' people. Tankass was an abbreviation for Town Council. Incidentally, if you wondered who the 'Piddle-de-dee' were, it was how the ordinary African pronounced the Public Works Department. Barbara has reminded me of the occasion when, one early morning, the bucket was withdrawn when she was in occupation!

While writing these lines about servants, I was reminded of being given a little book on my first tour entitled *A Household Book for Africa* by E. G. Bradley (1939). The lady who wrote this book lived in Tanganyika but her advice, clearly directed towards the European bachelor's household, was equally applicable to tropical West Africa. I will have to admit that in actual fact I made little use of the book, and indeed Gold Coast cooks needed little instruction in widening their cooking skills. The book, however, included a number of amusing little discourses between master and servant. The following is an example of one, and it is referred to as a Moral Tale, entitled 'Nothing to Eat'.

'Sir, what about dinner?'

'Well, cook, what have you got?'

'I got nothing, sir.'

'What, no meat?'

'No sir.'

'No chicken?'

'He is not dead.'

'No fish, no tin?'

'No sir.'

'What about vegetables?'

'Nothing sir, only spinach.'

'Let me see what there is in the safe.'

'A small piece of cheese, sir, two potatoes and two eggs.'

'Come, come, cook. This is luxury! I shall have . . .'

Then follow five quite attractive alternative menus incorporating spinach or potato soups, soufflés, omelettes, and even Welsh Rarebit.

A final remark from the master to the cook:

'Do not tell me there is nothing to eat!'

Some of the boys liked to play Warri when off duty. This was a game played all over West Africa. The wooden boards with rounded holes, into which pebbles were moved about, could be very crude, or neatly carved. The players would play very quickly, as Chinese would play Mah Jong. One or two Europeans claimed to play the game, saying that it was not so intricate as supposed. Probably few Europeans took the trouble to find out.

27

More Travels in the Gold Coast

It was a privilege that Government officials were allowed to take a short period of local leave once a tour. Despite this, during my nineteen years in the Gold Coast, I only took advantage of this opportunity twice. I am not sure whether this was due to devotion to duty or pressure of work! Believe it or not, we did work pretty hard in the Department of Agriculture, often taking work back to the bungalow to study over the evening's sundowner, and even getting up before dawn to finish off reports.

As I liked to travel extensively in the district, it was necessary to condense the office work into fewer hours on one's return. Paperwork was always abundant and reports were legion. There were monthly reports, quarterly reports, annual reports, foodstuff reports, staff reports, etc., etc. At the end of one's tour it was usual to write handing-over notes in great detail and take one's successor on a full tour of the district.

I took my first local leave while stationed at Kumasi – a tour of the Northern Territories. With a borrowed pick-up truck and my cook, we motored to Tamale, the capital, which I had not seen since my army days. After a day or two we journeyed north-eastward, visiting the agricultural stations at Navrongo and Bolgatanga. Conditions were extremely hot, though the Europeans in the north lived in bungalows of mud construction, and the very thick walls kept conditions reasonably cool and resisted termite attack.

From there we travelled on to Bawku at the north-eastern tip of the colony, and where we stayed in a very pleasant rest house. The climate here was so hot and dry that the thirsty expatriates actually added water to their Accra beer! Bawku was the entry point for the importation of cattle from the French colonies to the north, and this being the dry season, the assembly area seemed to lie in a permanent cloud of choking dust. As already described, these cattle were to walk all the way to the coast, any falling by the way being slaughtered at villages en route. The cattle were all of the Zebu type, having large humps, and in the case of the Ankole breed from Chad, very long horns. Incidentally, the hump is much prized as a delicacy, and I can confirm that it is very similar to tongue. The cattle trails to the north lead to such well-known towns as Ougadougo and further on still, the fabulous Timbukto, i.e. fabulous only as far as the name is concerned.

On the way home, we first travelled to the opposite north-west corner of the NTs, staying with the Agricultural Officer, L. F. Derraugh, at Lawra. On the way we passed Tumu, where the young District Commissioner was the only European for many miles around. Tumu rather fascinated me as it must have been one of the most lonely stations in the British Empire – again, shades of Somerset Maugham! The temptation to take up serious drinking must have been hard to resist!

After leaving Lawra we travelled through Savannah country, passing Wa, Bole and Kintampo and back to Kumasi. Camped at Bole we encountered a heavy drinking character always referred to as 'Deadeye Dick', and with whom we spent a convivial evening. Deadeye, a member of the Water Supply Department, having only one eye, impressed his Africans by placing his artificial eye over his money at the bedside each night. No African would ever take his money with his eye on it! We met Deadeye once again in Ashanti, and then he unexpectedly turned up on an Elder Dempster ship when we were going home on leave. Unfortunately he had omitted to bring a jacket and tie and was not allowed in to dinner. It probably didn't worry him too much as he preferred the bar and sandwiches.

For my other local leave I went down to the rest house at Big Ada at the mouth of the River Volta. I was accompanied by an agricultural friend, named Parsons. We stayed at the rest house, faring well on local fish and duck. Parsons had a sailing boat in which we explored the islands at the mouth of the River Volta. There was a long sandy beach within the bar from which it was pleasant to bathe. Normally I sat at the prow of the boat operating the jib sail, with Parsons at the stern and occupied with the mainsail and rudder and, at times, the outboard motor. There were many crocodiles along the banks of the river, usually disporting themselves in the sun, and one had to be careful when landing on some of the islands.

Parsons insisted that I should gain more experience by taking the boat out by myself. Rather nervously, but soon gaining confidence, I sailed off toward the river mouth, though hoping

The Volta River

141

that I should be able to turn around before being carried out to sea! However, I tacked around successfully, avoiding being knocked overboard by the mainsail, and was soon approaching Parsons again waiting for me on the shore, but however hard I tried, I was unable to sail in. Eventually I heard the shout, 'Put down your centre board!' That done, I sailed in without any further trouble! A feature of the Volta riverbanks was the many pied kingfishers hovering in the air before dropping like stones into the water after fish.

I found this holiday at Big Ada so idyllic that I rang my Deputy Director in Accra requesting an extension, but unfortunately to no avail. This Director was a Scotsman, James Broatch, who I got on very well with, and knew him after his retirement. Another Director, also a Scot, was D. H. Urquhart, whose visits to one's station were viewed with some trepidation . I always remember the advice of another Agricultural Officer, Wilbur Mason. It was, 'If asked a question, never say you don't know the answer. Say something, as the inquirer won't know!' I will briefly mention one other Director, who did not stay long, and was named Waters. When he arrived first he was referred to as 'Deep' Waters. Subsequently he became 'Still' Waters, and later still, 'Stagnant' Waters!

If an opportunity arose, Barbara and I would like to spend an odd night or two at Winneba, a seaside town about halfway between Accra and Cape Coast. The chief attraction of Winneba, at least for Europeans, was centred on a very friendly little club and an excellent swimming pool which had been cut out of the rocks on the beach. Every day it was refilled with sea water at high tide. Winneba was an important fishing centre, and it was always interesting to see the fishing fleet going out to sea each morning. Before reaching deeper water and putting up their sails, there would be an initial period of frenzied paddling through the surf. The boats returned again in the evening with the wind then blowing towards the shore. I tended to use Winneba as a base for visiting up-country centres, leaving the pool to Barbara and the children during the day. There were by now two children, Jonathan and Petrea.

I saw little of the western region during my time on the Gold Coast, but I did twice visit Wiawso in the far west, a rather remote station with half a dozen Europeans and a centre for cocoa production. Such a journey would be upwards of 200 miles, and prove tiring at the end of a long hot drive. However, after sitting down with a cold beer on arrival, and then a bath in a rest house or friend's bungalow, one quickly revived. It was in the Western Province of course that we passed the important gold mining towns of Tarkwa, Bibiani and the headquarters of the Ashanti goldfields at Obuasi.

While stationed at Accra, I was asked to visit Nigeria to report on a demonstration of Ferguson tractors to be held at Sameru, the agricultural station at Zaria in the north of the country. Massey Ferguson had then just brought out a range of small tractors that were to revolutionise the farming industry. It was thought that the use of these tractors would have some application in the cultivation of such crops as maize, millet and guinea corn in the northern regions of the Gold Coast. A feature of these tractors was the development of a three point linkage system which allowed the use of a range of easily fitted and subsequently easily detached implements and accessories.

The four days I spent in Nigeria gave me a most interesting mini-tour of that immense country. First, by air to Kano, where I spent a very hot and sticky night at the airport hotel. Kano was, and no doubt still is, a huge native city lying within its own walls. Here I saw the huge pyramids of bagged groundnuts, covered in black polythene and holding up to 1,000 tons in each. These pyramids had been erected as a wartime measure to preserve the nuts until transport became available to send them on their long journey to the coast. Shortage of shipping must have remained a continuing problem as the time of my visit was some time after the end of the war.

Trek to the Afram Plains

I travelled from Kano to Zaria by pick-up truck through countryside reminiscent of the Gold Coast Northern Territories, with yams one of the major crops. The tractor demonstration went off very well, and it was not long afterwards that all our cocoa stations were equipped with one of the small grey Fergie T.20 tractors, together with a trailer and other auxiliary equipment. After two nights in Zaria I travelled to Lagos, but with stops at the hill station of Jos and then Ibadan, said to be the most populous native city in Africa. I flew in a small single-engined Dove. These planes carried only eight passengers, and for most of the time I was the only occupant! There were fine views of the forest and savannah, and once a glimpse of the Niger showing up tea-brown far below. At Lagos I stayed in the very modern Olympic hotel, not long completed, and then back to Accra in a much larger plane. Flying as we did along the coast, there were splendid vistas of blue seas and the continuous coconut-lined sandy shores.

Another interesting trip worth a mention was a visit to the Afram Plains, a rather remote, thinly populated area lying in the north-east corner of the eastern region, with the River Volta marking the boundary with Togoland. I made this trek with an Agricultural Survey Officer, George Cooper, when I was stationed at Bunso. I thought of this trip as rather special, as the out-of-the-way nature of the country required the use of a Land Rover, and in the absence of rest houses we were obliged to take tents and camping equipment. I shall, however, have to use the past tense in describing the geography of the Afram Plains as they were then. The greater part of this area is now under water, and forming part of the great Volta river lake.

The Afram Plains that I visited covered an area of some 2,000 square miles and were bounded on three sides by the Volta river and its tributaries, the Afram and the Obosum. While there was some riverine forest which supported a few cocoa farms, the greater part of the area was covered with dwarf trees and elephant grass. The elephant grass could be six feet tall in the rainy season but in the dry season, which was the time we were there, most of the terrain had been burnt by hunters, and the 'trees' displayed the blackened, scarred bark of such fire-resistant species.

We crossed the Afram river by ford (clearly this could only be carried out in the dry season), where we encountered some particularly large and attentive tsetse flies. Then we set off for a village with the curious name of Bungalow. While we did encounter one or two mammy trucks, the road could only be described as 'difficult', perhaps an understatement, even for a Land Rover. On three occasions we had to cross bridges over deep dry stream beds. These bridges actually were comprised of loose planking, and it was essential for us passengers to get down while the driver timidly drove over, after undertaking considerable rearrangement of these materials. A ciné film I have graphically illustrates this.

I expect the village was called Bungalow because a European lived there once – only Europeans lived in bungalows! Anyway,

A Volta River Ferry

146

the children gave us a great welcome, and obviously did not see white men very often, though I must say there were several Roman Catholic priests living in the neighbourhood who shared some refreshment with us. Our driver and cook took to pitching the tent and preparing outdoor meals like ducks to water, and we seemed to have better meals than we could have had at home at Bunso. Barbara, who did not come with us, rather took exception to this, though I think eating out of doors has something to do with it! We spent some time on the banks of the Volta, still a large river at this point. There was plenty of activity with mammies and children bathing on the banks, and we took an interesting canoe trip. I was greatly impressed with the wealth of butterfly life, with swarms of swallowtails and other species congregating on wet patches along the roads. On our return journey the boys were very pleased to be able to purchase a 'cutting grass' – a large rodent resembling a big guineapig, and considered very fine 'chop' even by Europeans.

Towards the end of my sojourn in the Gold Coast, agricultural shows became popular. I recollect visiting shows at Bunso, Assuansi, Kpeve, and the largest of all at Tamale. The last show was extremely well attended, not only by the general public, but by local chiefs with their large umbrellas and retinues of retainers. Mounted Hausa and Fulani horsemen galloped around showing off their extravagant saddlery and harness. There were classes for sheep and goats and for farm produce such as yams, pumpkins, vegetables, etc. There were of course food stalls, palm wine bars, and donkey races in which the riders were required to sit facing the tail! Firms such as the United Africa Company had stands showing off modern, if perhaps at that time futuristic, farm machinery, as did of course the Department of Agriculture.

In the course of this book I have frequently referred to the liking of the colony's European population for the 'demon drink'. This was not necessarily a habit confined to parties, but a drink or two before meals was normal, whether or not one was in the company of friends. One should remember that the climate was hot, one's companions were comparatively young and enthusiastic, and there was in place a tradition of bonhomie and entertaining. Despite this, nearly everyone worked hard, and as far as I was concerned I have no recollection of ever arriving late in the office in the morning after a night out.

While during my time on the Coast I met many socially heavy drinkers, there were few who could be termed alcoholics. I have elsewhere referred to Deadeye Dick, but another strange character was Spud Mullan of my own department. I met him first at Assuansi when he surprised me by taking several large gins before playing tennis – this, he explained, enabled him to see the ball with greater clarity! His nationality will be made clear from his habit of referring to the Orangemen, the Apprentice Boys, and the Battle of the Boyne. His favourite utterance was, 'Hell roast the Pope.'

Later on, when we were both stationed at Accra, he was always sending over his steward boy at breakfast time to 'borrow' a bottle of cold beer and a razor blade. When he visited me once in my bungalow in Togoland, accompanied by his African girlfriend who had acquired the Irish name of Elana, he proved a difficult though likeable guest. It would seem however, that Spud's usefulness to the department deteriorated, and one day in Accra he unexpectedly disappeared from the scene. Afterwards we heard that our Director, James Broatch, had arranged that he should be sent home quietly by air without any fuss or disciplinary action. We did hear later through the grapevine that Spud, having returned to the Emerald Isle (the northern section of course), had became a reformed character, and worked as a cattle inseminator.

Cocoa Spraying Gangs

Dehusking Cocoa Pods

Cocoa beans drying in the sun

28

The Cocoa Industry in the Gold Coast

The cultivation of cocoa in the Gold Coast dates back only as far as the late nineteenth century, and then there were no appreciable exports until after the First World War. History records that the introduction of this South American tree occurred with the import of a single cocoa pod about the year 1878 via Fernando Po. Production peaked in the 1930s with output varying between 200,000 and 275,000 tons per annum, and with a record tonnage of 311,000 tons reached in 1936. The Gold Coast, latterly Ghana, established itself in this century as a premier producer of cocoa, and at a time of its peak production its output was about a third of the whole world's. In the period 1949–53 the FOB* value of cocoa exports from the Gold Coast averaged £52 million per annum, representing two thirds of all domestic exports.

Cocoa cultivation in the Gold Coast has always been a purely peasant grown crop on innumerable small farms, often adjoining and spread over a large part of the closed forest areas where conditions were favourable for its growth. There was also some production in riverine situations in more marginal savannah areas. While individuals might own a number of small farms, these were usually fragmented and their boundaries ill-defined. Some larger farmers might emply a few labourers, usually from the

*FOB = Free on board.

151

Northern Territories, but generally the individual farmer would carry out the necessary cultivations himself with the aid of his family. To be productive, cocoa farms were planted in areas of adequate rainfall and under the shade of large haphazardly growing forest trees. The beans were not planted in straight rows but at random spacings. Despite the comparative smallness of individual farms, in favoured areas one could walk mile after mile through continuous cocoa.

The purchase of cocoa was always made in loads of 60 lb weight. Prices varied steeply from year to year, though there was a steady rise from as low as 10/- to 15/- a load before the war to as high as 70/- to 80/- a load in the 1950s. While I originally supervised the marketing of a large proportion of the crop through the cooperatives, sales through other organisations were also widespread. The larger agents included Cadbury and Fry, Lyons, the United Africa Company and G. B. Ollivants. These firms had numerous agents and sub-agents dotted about the bush. The main buying time was from September to January, with a minor crop in mid season. Before the crop is marketed the beans have to be prepared. After the pods were harvested they were dehusked, allowing the slimy beans to be fermented in heaps, later to be dried in the sun on raised platforms. The Department of Agriculture ran a very comprehensive grading service at the ports, and no cocoa beans could be exported without full inspection.

During my early years on the Gold Coast, it became apparent that all was not well with the health of the cocoa industry. Even in the most suitable growing districts, large areas seemed to be dying out. Symptoms exhibited were obscure leaf mosaics, and at times swollen stems and chupons, hence the adoption of the malady's name as Swollen Shoot. It was clear that the disease was of virus origin, though even with the nearby presence of the experts of the Cocoa Research Station at Tafo, it was some years before the puzzle of the disease's cause was solved. Trees infected with the more virulent strains of Swollen Shoot suffered rapid decline, with death in as little as three years.

As an interim measure it was decided to combat the spread of the disease by a cutting-out campaign. This involved the eradication of all symptom-carrying trees with compensation only latterly payable to farmers. This necessitated the inspection of cocoa farms over huge areas, and ultimately involved payments running into millions of pounds. Payments would vary according to tree size, with 4/- the amount for the largest.

With cocoa still maintaining a reasonable price, the removal of symptom-showing but still bearing trees was often an unpopular measure, and at times led to trouble between the farmers and the African junior staff. Felled tree trunks were piled in heaps for subsequent rocording, and there was of course the ever-present risk of financial 'jiggery-pokery' occurring. It was to be a few years after the end of the war (1946) that Peter Posnette of WACRI finally got to the bottom of the problem. I knew Peter Posnette well and he eventually came to be the head of the East Malling Research Station in Kent.

The term Swollen Shoot was found to cover a number of separate viruses which differed in severity, mosaic symptoms and the absence or otherwise of swollen shoots. It was found that the carriers of the disease were mealy bugs (pseudococcus spp.). While these are wingless creatures, they are normally attended by ants which move them about. Mealy bugs were known to be endemic in forest areas, and common trees such as the large silk cotton were found to harbour them. Transmission within cocoa was found to be normally only from tree to tree, particularly where the canopies intertwine.

The possibility of eliminating mealy bugs in West African cocoa farms appeared to be a non-starter. The only solution seemed to be a continuation and sharpening up of the established roguing policy in combination with a replanting campaign. It would have seemed desirable to have concentrated rehabilitation in regions free of old and diseased cocoa trees, and particularly in new areas altogether. Unfortunately, land not yet planted with cocoa was becoming more and more limited, and where cocoa had largely died out, the 'slash and burn' treatment of the remaining undergrowth for food farms tended to produce a micro-climate unsuitable for the profitable production of cocoa. As a result semi-forest areas were decreasing, particularly from the south and east, while the influence of the Sahara encroached a little more each year from the north.

The timber trade has tended to earn itself a bad name where deforestation is concerned. At that time, however, I could not seriously blame it for these climatic changes. It removed only trees of economic worth which, as shade trees in the cocoa, were spread around with perhaps only one or two to the hectare. These trees were bought and felled individually and hauled out by tractor, usually leaving enough large trees of less economic species to maintain a suitable micro-climate in the cocoa. As already noted, however, where cocoa had died out, shifting cultivation for food crops had tended to produce conditions less suitable for cocoa production. More satisfactorily, it may be mentioned that the Forestry Department had established reserves in strategic parts of the closed forest zones to assist in the maintenance of stable climatic conditions and rainfall distribution. No food farming or other agricultural activity were allowed in these reserves, though what happened after the commencement of self-government I am not so sure.

It will be seen from the foregoing that the future of Ghana as a premier cocoa producer was in grave danger. With the necessity of handing over the ex-colony in good financial shape, it was decided to introduce an even more extensive campaign to rehabilitate the industry.

29

The Cocoa Industry. 1954–58
Disease Control

The future of cocoa in Ghana remained in some doubt in the 1950s. While there were also substantial exports of palm products, timber, bauxite and gold, cocoa remained by far the major export commodity, and indeed it could be said to represent the lifeblood of the country. In 1947 three virologists – afterwards to be known as the Three Wise Men – visited the colony to assess the disease position and recommend measures of control. Their main conclusions were that we should have to live with the disease, and there were no alternatives to cutting out.

To combat this now serious threat, a new and separate division of the department was formed in the early 1950s with a Deputy Director in charge with headquarters in Accra. The field campaign was to be in the hands of another new appointment, the Assistant Director of Cocoa Agronomy and Training (ADA CAT for short) with headquarters at Bunso in the eastern region. The initial appointment of ADA CAT was Phil Hammond, and it was from him that I took over for my last two tours. Phil Hammond, MBE, was an officer for whom I had tremendous respect. His knowledge of cocoa and all its problems was profound, and after his retirement he continued to visit Ghana and other cocoa growing countries as a consultant. If Phil Hammond had a fault at all, it was to attend to even the minutest details himself. To this day I refer to modern fruit growers, or others who have an exhaustive knowledge, of their subject as 'Phil Hammonds'! I eventually became ADA CAT.

To carry out this huge disease and rehabilitation programme required the appointment of an additional grade of senior officer – the Agricultural Survey Officer (ASO for short). By 1954 there were no fewer than 150 ASOs in position, headed by five principal ASOs. While a number of the original appointees were expatriates, latterly they were mainly Africans. Some idea of the immensity of the programme, both financially and administratively, can be appreciated when it is understood that each ASO had a staff of about 30 junior field assistants, each of whom controlled a number of labourers. In fact in the 137 designated districts, the total number of field assistants amounted to 4,500.

ASOs as senior officers were entitled to bungalows, all of which had to be constructed in rural areas by a newly-formed departmental works branch, and quite independently of the Public Works Department. The ADA at Bunso continued to meet and often entertain an increasingly wide circle of VIP visitors.

As ADA CAT, I was responsible for all cocoa growing in the country, with, in addition, one week a month away in Trans Volta/Togoland on general agricultural duties, and staying at Kpeve. It was always my practice not to become office-bound, and I continued to spend nights away in rest houses while visiting Swollen Shoot outbreaks, cocoa stations etc. Inspection work was not always by road transport, and in my time I must have walked many hundreds of miles along bush paths through the forest, sometimes crossing streams over fallen tree trunks or, where such aids were not available, carried through the water by hefty labourers. Barbara remarks that I was lighter in those days!

I have already referred to the Swollen Shoot cutting-out

campaign and the detailed surveying and mapping carried out in all cocoa-growing areas. Other work centred on Bunso involved:

a) The establishment and subsequent maintenance of some twenty 100-acres or more cocoa stations spread throughout the main cocoa growing districts, and including one or two stations on the fringes of less suitable growing areas.
b) The provision of a large number of strategically-placed nurseries capable of growing and supplying quantities of improved cocoa planting material to be used in the rehabilitation campaign.
c) The training of staff who were to supervise and carry out all the extension work, and to provide facilities for subsequent refresher courses;
d) The study and experimental work on pests and diseases other than Swollen Shoot, and which might have a bearing on the profitable cultivation of cocoa in West Africa.

Apart from Bunso being the headquarters of the works branch, there was also the presence of a large transport division. Each district office had to provide drawing-office facilities, and was required to deal with a lot of paying out. At all times, of course, a close liaison was maintained with the specialist officers at the West African Cocoa Research Unit nearby.

It was becoming apparent that there was a secondary hazard threatening the cocoa crop. The leaf canopy of cocoa farms over large areas, and particularly in the eastern region, was being adversely affected by capsids, and this at times was causing severe defoliation. Considerable experimental work was carried out to combat this pest, and subsequently with the assistance of the firm of Plant Protection Ltd. This was the time that the two insecticides DDT and GAMMA BHC were being introduced into the United Kingdom, and it was soon established that both chemicals were efficient in combating cocoa capsid, and indeed a range of other pests, including the anopheles mosquito. It was some years later that DDT was withdrawn for exhibiting certain undesirable properties, though GAMMA BHC maintained its position as an efficient and reasonably cheap capsid eradicator.

In the course of our rehabilitation work Plant Protection Ltd proceeded to bring out further recently-discovered chemicals for trial. These included the organo-phosphorous insecticides Aldrin, Dieldren and Endrin. All these have now been barred from use, and Endrin in particular has proved especially toxic. By this time a large-scale operation had been mounted against the cocoa capsid, and this involved the saturation spraying of huge tracts of cocoa using motorised knapsack sprayers. With the cooperation of Plant Protection some 600 Motorblos had been imported. Sections of five labourers, each one armed with a Motorblo, marched through the cocoa farms spraying upwards into the canopy. Another labourer with a sixth machine walked behind in reserve ready to fill in if any breakdown occurred. Many years afterwards, I did wonder whether any of these operators had been affected in any way from exposure to these potentially poisonous chemicals. Nowadays of course full suits of protective clothing would have been worn.

The use of all this mechanical equipment necessitated considerable back-up, and this was carried out from a depôt at Bunso staffed by several Plant Protection personnel. The formulation of 'Gammalin 20' was proving the most efficient and economical to be used, and at one time, the department were saturation-spraying as a routine measure upwards of 100,000 acres of cocoa farms The improvement in the health of farms was most marked, and it is possibly as a result of this that a record cocoa crop of 549,000 tons was produced in the 1964/65 season. In addition to the power-driven knapsack sprayers, thousands of small 'mysto' pneumatic sprayers were sold to the farmers at a subsidised price of £2 each with chemicals free of charge. The use of these latter machines was largely directed to the spraying of young cocoa planted during the course of the rehabilitation campaign. They were also useful for spraying the copper fungicide 'Perenox' against blackpod disease, and also for combating termites which could be a problem on young cocoa recently planted in the more marginal districts.

The distribution of superior planting material continued on a massive scale, involving at times the free lining out and pegging of farms. In the year 1954/55 direct expenditure on the cocoa industry amounted to no less than £3,228,000. This is a lot of money nowadays, but was astronomical in those times. With full self-government just around the corner, no one could say that the British Government were not doing their best to leave the country on a sound footing.

The type of cocoa normally grown in West Africa was almost 100% of the rather small-podded Amelonado variety. It was highly desirable that higher-yielding types should be introduced to quicken up the rehabilitation campaign. Some hundred clones of large-podded Amazon selections had been under experimental scrutiny at Bunso, and from these, the ten most promising clones had been chosen for further multiplication on the numerous cocoa nurseries. The fungus disease blackpod could be a significant problem in the wetter areas, but its seriousness had little impact when compared to the depredations of Swollen Shoot and capsid. One serious complaint that I observed in Trinidad and Grenada, 'Witch's Broom', was fortunately absent in West Africa.

As I have mentioned already, the satisfactory growth of native cocoa farms was largely dependent on the shade and protection of large forest trees. Often, however, these trees grew too large or were too dense and thus affected the cocoa. Then some thinning became desirable. The department had perfected a way of carrying this out by 'frilling' the trunks of the larger trees and then treating the cuts with sodium arsenite. Later experimental work showed that it was only necessary to paint the unbroken bark with a hormone arboricide such as 245T in the proprietary formulation

'Trioxone'. This treatment was so effective that large forest trees treated in March 1954, for instance, were dead by June 1955. The subsequent disintegration of the dead trees did not prove as hazardous as might have been thought. They did not fall all at once but dropped to the ground piece by piece.

Cocoa Nursery

Plantation scene

30

The Cocoa Industry. Later Developments

While I had formally retired in mid-1958, it had always been my intention to return to Ghana to continue the cocoa work on a contract basis. I had also discussed with Sir Geoffrey Nye, the Colonial Office Agricultural Adviser, the possibility of agricultural work in other countries. Vacancies mentioned were the director-ships of Sierra Leone and British Honduras. However, having purchased a small farm near Ledbury in Herefordshire and started to plant up apple trees, I gradually distanced myself from these ideas. Moreover, in the course of time, I was able to purchase several lots of adjoining land, ultimately bringing the size of the farm to some 115 acres.

I regret to say that it was only when I came round to writing these present chapters on my African experiences that I became curious to know what had happened to the cocoa industry since those days. This interest was sharpened when an old departmental colleague, Roy Silverlock, described to me a holiday visit he had made to Ghana in 1992. He did paint a rather dismal picture of a road trip he made from Accra to Kumasi, on which he saw only a few patches of forest trees and a preponderance of secondary bush and food farms with very little cocoa showing up. His opinion was that the main areas of cocoa production were now mainly in the western region and western Ashanti. He visited Bunso and what was WACRI but is now CRIG (Cocoa Research Institute of Ghana). Both institutions he said were very run-down.

This information led me to investigate some of the fortunes of the cocoa industry since I was last there in 1958. Phil Hammond's exhaustive reports provided abundant information on this. It is recorded that between 1945/46 and 1961/62 a total of 112,366,000 infected and contact cocoa trees had been cut out and removed by the department during the course of the disease campaign. Despite this control had not been fully obtained and Swollen Shoot had continued to spread and reappear. What was more encouraging, however, was that some 50%–60% of the area treated had been replanted. By 1962 the new government were starting to feel the pinch financially and it was decided to disband the cocoa division, leaving the farmers to deal with the disease themselves. Apart from this, free spraying had been discontinued in 1959, though machines and chemicals were still available at subsidised prices. As can be imagined, as a result of this the position worsened, and the spread of the disease increased.

Accordingly, in 1965 the cocoa division was reinstated, though no grant payments were to be made and cutting-out was to be voluntary. With regard to spraying, while some resistance by pests to some of the insecticides used had been reported, the importation and the scale of mistblowers' spare parts, chemicals, etc. had become big business, and contractors for both spraying and workshop facilities were becoming very busy. 1970 saw the start of the 'plant as you cut' scheme. Cutting-out would still be at the farmers' expense, but hybrid seedling cocoa plants were given out free and replanted cocoa was maintained, also free of charge, for three years. Attempts to restart the saturation spraying of capsid outbreaks failed due to poor organisation, lack of funds, and latterly a shortage of imports.

It can be visualised from the foregoing that, for a period of

162

some thirty years, disease control and rehabilitation work on cocoa in Ghana was a very stop-go affair. Despite the fact that Ghana has emerged as one of the brighter spots among the ex-African colonies, it has had its times of instability and impecuniosity. Even before self-government, the size of cocoa crops and world prices would fluctuate from year to year. In years of very low prices the farmer would tend to neglect his farm, or even abandon it, or if the price was better in the adjoining country he would smuggle his crop over the frontier. As an illustration how prices can vary, in 1977 the price of cocoa rose to over three times what it was in 1972. After that it fell until in 1990 it was only half its 1972 price.

Despite continual difficulties Ghana remained the leading world producer of cocoa as far as tonnage is concerned until 1978, with a peak production of 557,000 tons in 1956. By 1978, however, production had slumped to 300,000 tons per annum, and then in 1983 adverse conditions and drought had reduced the crop to an all-time low of 185,000 tons. This was the year when a serious epidemic of bush fires affected extensive areas of cocoa, particularly in the eastern region. One can only attribute such unusual fires to climatic changes caused by reduction of forest tree cover and intensified food production. At one time, tropical forests were said to cover 34% of the country, but now the forest is reduced to only a quarter of its original size. Later the Ivory Coast has overtaken Ghana as the largest producer of cocoa, and Brazil has also competed very closely. After the débâcle in 1983, the government steadily increased prices for the farmer, and between that time and the present day production has averaged out at between 250,000 and 300,000 tons per annum. The average price for a ton of cocoa was said to be £866 in 1995, which I presume to be a FOB quotation.

31

The British Empire

It is a sad reflection of present day times that so often one can only read criticism of our former British Empire. Indeed, one might have thought that the Empire was governed by a Colonel Blimp, who, apart from swallowing chota pegs and massacring wild life, lorded it over the natives who were ruthlessly exploited in the name of capitalism. While this of course represents a very extreme scenario, I do wonder myself how the subject of the Empire is dealt with in present day school and university syllabuses.

One of course must emphasise that the very opposite of these sentiments is true, and we should take pride in the fact that the British Empire has been one of the greatest forces for human progress that the world has ever seen. Even Nelson Mandela, having been imprisoned for many years, said when he recently visited this country:

'I was brought up in a British school, and at that time Britain was the home of everything that was best in the world. I have not discarded the influence which Britain and British history and culture exercised on us.'

It is a long time since the days of the slave trade, when indeed Europeans did go out to Africa to trade and exploit the African. It is worth remembering, however, that the individual who did the

164

most to bring this evil trade to an end was an Englishman, William Wilberforce. Foremost among the explorers and missionaries was another Englishman, Livingstone. He brought to the notice of the world the horrors of the Arab slave trade in Central and East Africa, so providing the impetus for its extinction of slavery there also.

Possibly the greatest influence in promoting the British Empire, in Nigeria and Uganda in particular, could be attributed to Lord Lugard (1858–1945). Wherever he went in Africa and elsewhere he was responsible for promoting the British way of life with its belief in justice, individual freedom and representative government. His doctrine was that Europe was in Africa, not only for the benefit of its own people, but equally for the native races in their progress towards self-determination. This is said to be a quotation of his:

'For two or three generations we can show the Negro what we are. Then we shall be asked to go away. Then we shall leave the land to those it belongs to, with the feeling that they have better business friends in us than in other white men.'

Before discussing the situation in West Africa, and in the Gold Coast in particular, I must say a few words about the 'Scramble for Africa'. In the latter years of the nineteenth century and afterwards, Great Britain vied with France, Germany, Belgium and Portugal to take over and settle vast expanses of Africa south of the Sahara. In those days, the more open lands of southern and central Africa were inhabited by many diverse tribes spread comparatively thinly over the country. By European standards these tribes were very primitive and their numbers kept down by tribal warfare and disease. There were indeed quite large tracts of land with few or no inhabitants, and it could be justifiably argued that European settlers had every right to take over such uninhabited terrain.

After the First World War the Germans disappeared from the scene, leaving the French, Belgians and the Portuguese, together with the British, as the competing colonial powers south of the equator. While it became the set intention of the British eventually to hand over their acquired territories as self-governing entities, the other Europeans had in mind a more 'what we have, we hold' policy, with their colonies remaining for all time under their own sovereign powers. The French were the keenest with such sentiments, and though they were not very successful with their African colonies, to this day the islands of Martinique and Guadeloupe in the Caribbean are departments in the French Parliament.

In the case of the British colonies in Africa, there has always been some distinction between west and east. The West African colonies of the Gold Coast, the Gambia, Nigeria and Sierra Leone have always been referred to as 'blackman countries'. They were described as such as their potentially hot and unhealthy climates made it suitable for Europeans to come out to work and trade, but not to settle after retirement. The establishment of large European-run plantations has never been encouraged in British West Africa. Some of the more tropical East African colonies also came into this category including Uganda, Tanganyika (now Tanzania) and Nyasaland (now Malawi).

Kenya and Rhodesia (now Zimbabwe) were at one time considered rather differently, as the fertile and healthy Highlands had largely been occupied by white settlers who lived among the itinerant Masai and the wild animals. Often with very little capital and resources they carved farms out of the bush, and as more and more settlers arrived, it became the intention that Kenya would become an independent country with Nairobi an impressive capital. I will agree that there developed in Kenya a minority of happy-go-lucky Europeans who included the 'pretty people' of the Muthaiga Club set. I have made reference to the Earl of Erroll scandal in my wartime Nairobi account, though I am sure that after the incidence of the Mau Mau and the last war, such goings on no longer existed.

British recruits for the colonial service were usually young public school and university trained men. The basic unit of British rule was the District Commissioner (Gold Coast) or the District Officer (Nigeria) who were often responsible for the supervision of territories as large as small countries. They became used to working in lonely bush stations and among primitive peoples and tribes, and were required to attain an adequate knowledge of local customs and languages. As the Lugard tradition dictated, the people were governed through their chiefs, a custom well understood by the population and appealing of course to the chiefs themselves. This was technically the 'Divide and Rule' system which allowed small numbers of officers to control large numbers of people spread over equally large areas. British Colonial Officers were almost invariably people of the highest integrity, and this was well understood by the population. Gifts to Government Officers were normally reimbursed in kind, and during all the time I served in West Africa I was never once offered a bribe. It is sad to think that once self-government had been attained, most of the newly-born countries became bywords for 'bribery and corruption'.

It has been said that by treating their colonial peoples with such enlightenment, and encouraging education and progress, the British signed their own eviction orders. When, after the war, demands for self-government became overwhelming, Britain allowed this self-determination to go ahead with little or no obstruction. While with hindsight progress was certainly too rapid, events did not end up in tears, or in fact bloodshed, as was experienced by the Belgians and Portuguese. In more recent times, however, events in Nigeria and Sierra Leone in particular have resulted in these two countries very seriously blotting their copybooks. Liberia, a country never colonised, suffered even worse disruption.

While I have been referring to the break-up of the British Empire, there nowadays seems to be a movement towards the partial break-up of the United Kingdom. While I was serving in the colonies, and also in the army, I had very many acquaintances and friends from all parts of the British Isles. While some might talk with different accents, and some be referred to as Jock or Paddy, I always considered everybody to be equal and all members of one great family. It now seems that sections of these geographical entities are looking forward to some sort of autonomy – also known as devolution – and there are indeed some elements in Scotland who appear to favour complete separation.

Writing in late 1997, I am sorry to report that devolution was then well under way in both Scotland and Wales, though in the latter case only some 25% of the population actually voted in favour of the move. With more and more emphasis on our becoming fully amalgamated with the Common Market, I am sure that it would have been preferable that the United Kingdom should remain fully united rather than become a partnership of fragmented pieces.

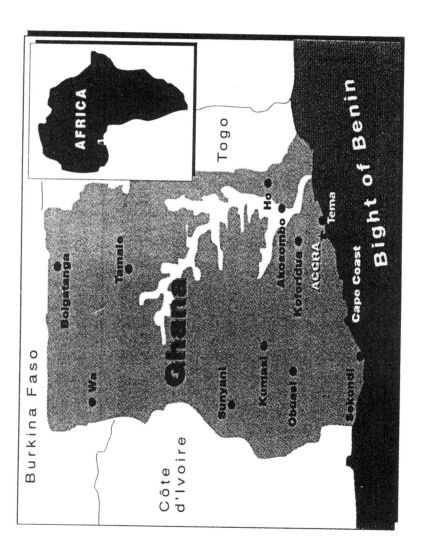

The distribution of the Volta River Lake in present day Ghana (1998)

32

The Transition.
The Gold Coast to Ghana

In the last chapter I discussed the British Empire as a whole, and Africa in particular. Now I wish to give attention to the Gold ' Coast alone. When I first went there in April 1939, I arrived in a happy, well-governed colony. I was to learn that it was the ultimate intention of Great Britain to train and educate the population towards a goal of eventual self-government. While it might be conceded that this was proceeding at a somewhat leisurely pace, the people seemed well satisfied with their lot, and generally showed no marked aspirations towards accelerated self-determination. In fact the colony was a rich one with valuable exports of cocoa, timber, gold, diamonds, manganese and various minor products. As far as I was aware, the mother country did not absorb any of the profits which were reinvested in the Gold Coast's economy.

Was there a colour bar, or did our occupation amount to racialism? Definitely not! Even by 1949 the European population was no more than 4,000 to 5,000. As far as the government service was concerned, the Africans were either senior of junior officers, thought it might be conceded that there were not many of the former, and in the Agricultural Department, very few indeed. As

170

I have already explained, African senior officers were the equivalent of their European counterparts – they had bungalows, car allowances and similar wage scales. Africanisation was perhaps most marked in the legal and medical professions and, apart from lawyers, there were a number of fully-fledged judges and magistrates. While the much more numerous junior African officers were always treated in a fair and friendly way, they necessarily existed on a somewhat lower plane. In fact you did not ask junior officers to dinner.

If there could be any criticism of the British, it might be that they tended to keep to themselves rather than to mix socially with Africans. After a hard day's work in a hot and enervating climate, the typical Englishman liked to relax on his veranda in the evening, or attend the club for drinks at the bar or a game of snooker. When the European clubs were open to all-comers very few Africans seemed to want to join, and certainly none of the Syrian, Lebanese or Indian communities. While Africans and Europeans lived together very amicably, their lifestyles tended to differ, particularly as regards food and social habits. The better-off Africans with larger bungalows tended to open their doors to many visitors, and their poorer relations were always free to invade their hospitality.

When I have in recent years travelled on cruise ships and have gone ashore in tropical countries with other passengers, the latter would often show great surprise at the living conditions, particularly in the poorer areas. 'Oh, the poverty!' they would exclaim. They did not realise that to live in tropical climes is so very different from our cold conditions. The weather is nearly always warm, so a minimum expenditure on clothes is required. Bathing and cooking can be carried out in the compound out of doors, and food is usually cheaply available in the local marketplace. Family relationships are normally very close so that poorer members are usually looked after by those more fortunate. Nobody starves in West Africa or the West Indies.

When the war came to an end, there was no reason to imagine

171

that things would not go on as before. The Gold Coast was still looked upon as a model colony, relatively prosperous and future self-government assured, though this was to be brought in slowly and steadily. In 1946 no one would have dreamt that the Gold Coast was to become independent within a decade.

At first the forerunners in the Gold Coast of eventual independence were a group of middle-class Africans, mainly lawyers, and dominated by the influential Dr Danquah. Their party was known as the United Gold Coast Convention Party, (the UGCC). As a group they were generally sympathetic to the British way of life, and were prepared to proceed towards self-government at a reasonable pace. In 1947, however, the situation radically changed. This was when the young Kwame Nkrumah returned to the colony after an absence of a number of years abroad. He was appointed secretary of the UGCC, and from that time the whole situation changed. Nkrumah had very different priorities and he adopted a much more belligerent approach.

Another factor that was becoming apparent was the attitude of the 30,000 ex-servicemen population. Although they had been so cooperative and well disciplined as soldiers, they had become worldly wise during their service abroad and had brought back new ideas as to how their country was to be run in the future. The position blew up in 1948 when a misunderstanding occasioned the police to open fire on a demonstrating mob. This resulted in several casualties and three days of rioting ensued.

The UGCC then became the Convention People's Party (the CPP) and while the fore-mentioned founder members of the UGCC still adopted a conciliatory attitude, Kwame Nkrumah went about making as much mischief as possible. A classic turnabout of events followed when the Governor, Sir Arden Clarke, committed Nkrumah to prison, only to let him out again in 1949 when he gave him the appointment of 'Leader of Government Business'. Events then galloped on with Africans, usually with very limited knowledge and experience, being appointed ministers. The British civil servants carried on as usual, and largely in the capacity of advisers, though the work of the Agricultural Department showed few changes. I will not go into detail about this transition period, but full self-government was declared in 1957 with Nkrumah as President. I myself left Ghana in 1958 on pension.

One of Nkrumah's first acts was to allow imprisonment without trial, and apart from building up a cult of his personality, he organised a ruthless one-party police state. In 1960 he declared the country a republic, by which time he had moved into Christiansborg Castle as president. This sequence of events typified the rise to power of several other dictators of ex-African colonies.

While all this was going on, two very important projects were being planned in Ghana – the construction of a deep water port at Tema some 30 miles along the coast from Accra, to be followed by the building of the Akosombo Dam on the Volta river at a point some 40 miles north of the capital. The purpose of the dam was to provide hydro-electric power on a grand scale for running an aluminium smelter at Tema, and also to cover the power needs of the whole of the rest of the country, including the mining industry.

The dam was finally completed in 1966, and behind it materialised a vast lake, some 3,275 square miles in extent, and in fact the largest man-made lake in the world, though by capacity only the fourth. While the full extent of the lake measured some 250 miles from north to south, its shape was not a regular one, but formed a number of tentacles along the various tributary valleys including the Oti, the Afram and the Black Volta, in addition to the main river. It took until 1968 for the lake to reach its peak level of 270 feet. The human problems were immense, as some 80,000 people had to be settled elsewhere. A further dam of some size was also established at Kpong some miles downstream of Akosombo. Apart from the hydro-electric programme, there was also a scheme to provide large scale irrigation for the Accra plains in the interest of increased food production.

As can be imagined the costs were immense and required the

introduction of a lot of capital from other countries, the USA in particular. Despite the fact that it was incumbent on Nkrumah to keep in with his financiers, his mismanagement was gradually bringing the economy of the country to a low ebb. This gave the financing companies the whip hand to a great extent, and they insisted in giving priority to the aluminium smelter at Tema, which was the property of the Volta River Aluminium Company (VALCO). In the first place it was to treat imported bauxite rather than that produced in the country itself. The proposed irrigation scheme for the Accra plains also had to be abandoned.

Then in 1966 came a big surprise. While Kwame Nkrumah was away on a visit to China a military rising took place in Ghana, effectively deposing him, and as a result he never returned. K. A. Busia, an African civilian of the old school, took over the government from 1969 to 1972, but his administration was weak and an army officer, Colonel Achempong then organised a second coup d'état. He instituted a rapacious régime that lasted from 1972 to 1978. He was finally ousted by Flight Lieutenant Jerry Rawlings who had Achempong shot for corruption. If this had been Liberia or Nigeria I would have accepted this brutality, but not Ghana. NO! Like many other Europeans I have thought of the Ghanaians as some of the kindliest and most pleasant people in the whole of Africa. Rawlings, however, has continued to govern Ghana up to the present time. His régime has been reasonably enlightened, and Ghana can now be considered one of the more successful African nations.

I will return once more to the lake. After it had reached full capacity, supplies of electricity became sufficient to allow some export of power to neighbouring Togo and Dahomey (later Benin), and there were even more ambitious schemes to export to the Ivory Coast and elsewhere. Supplies of fish seemed to build up from nowhere in the lake and fishing soon became a prominent occupation, while water transport on the lake, though mainly on a small scale, increased. The fishermen were mainly of the Tongu

174

tribe from the south, and they settled all around the lakeside. I must mention here the nightmare capacity of the lake to spread disease. Between 1961 and 1964 the dread Bilharzia spread from 5% to 90% of the lakeside children, and within a few years, the whole 4,000 miles of shoreline became infected wherever there were people. The incidence of river blindness (onchocerciasis) also became widespread, though I believe modern drugs are now proving effective against both these scourges.

Then a further unexpected turn of events occurred in the 1970s. The Sahelian drought that commenced in 1971 led to a gradual lowering of the water in the lake, and by 1982 the level had dropped from 270 to 249 feet, which was close to the minimum operating level. The VALCO aluminium smelter at Tema suffered reduced consumption in stages, and came to a complete halt in November, 1983. There is no doubt that the droughts experienced can be attributed to the southward creep of the Sahara desert, possibly combined with the reduction of rain forest areas in Ghana.

Like other small African states, Ghana suffered a number of economic problems during its early years of independence. Despite its large exports of cocoa, timber, etc., the country was always dependent on imports of oil and foodstuffs. Prices of export commodities have varied widely over the years and inflation has usually been present, often seriously so. However, under the rule of Jerry Rawlings things have recently improved. The formerly state-dominated economy had been reformed, and though inflation still rears its ugly head, there has in the last year or two been an encouraging improvement in organisation and some useful privatisation. Britain remains Ghana's principal trading partner, and it is said that British interests have invested £500 million in Ghana, mainly in the mining, construction, banking and manu-facturing sectors. No doubt since the breakdown of the Eastern European bloc Ghana has become more capitalistic minded, and indeed Ghana may now be considered a star in sub-Sarahan Africa and should have a bright future.

Returning once more to the days of Kwame Nkrumah, there is no doubt that he must be blamed for the problems that have beset this potentially rich country, the first 'colony' to be 'liberated' in 1957. The bigger irony is that forty years ago the Gold Coast was really flourishing under colonial rule. When the British left Ghana they left a country with a balance of payments surplus, a well-trained administration, an independent judiciary and a steeply falling death rate. After a decade of Kwame 'the Redeemer' Nkrumah's rule the country had become a backward, disease-ridden ruin.

Kwame Nkrumah (1909–1972), although born in the Gold Coast, was educated in Pennsylvania and afterwards at the London School of Economics. He was a devoted Marxist, but like others of his kind made a practice of feathering his own nest. After being deposed by the army while he was in Peking he never returned to Ghana, but sought refuge with the loathsome Sekon Touré of Guinea and finally died of cancer in Bucharest.

The energy situation in Ghana at the time of writing (1997) is not altogether clear. It would seem that supplies of water from the dams still remain below par, with the result that there is still a shortage of hydro-electric power for the requirements of the VALCO smelter and general business and household needs. There have been two recent developments that may assist matters. Explorations along the coastal shelf have located the sources of both oil and gas. An oil refinery in the Tema area is already in limited production, as is gas from the offshore Tano gas fields in the western region. The construction of a thermal plant (to run on oil or gas) was started by the Volta River Authority in 1994 and is said to be due for completion in 1998. It is intended that it should run on either gas from the Tano gas fields or on oil, possibly piped from Nigeria. Finance is being made available from the World Bank. Further to all this there are plans to construct another hydro-electric dam at Bui on the Black Volta, and this venture should provide power for the needs of the Northern Territories.

I considered it to be a great compliment to Ghana when in 1997 Kofi Annan was appointed Secretary General of the United Nations, a most prestigious post. It does not say a lot, however, for the research capabilities of a number of television broadcasters and commentators who have continued to this day (September 1997) to pronounce the common African name of Kofi as Koffee! He was, of course, born on a Friday.

33

Apple Trees and Banana Boats

While it was formerly my intention to resume work in the Gold Coast on a contractual basis, it happened that the house we had purchased at Ledbury in Herefordshire was centred on a rundown fruit farm of 19 acres. Once we had enthusiastically started planting the land up with new apple trees, it became difficult to go back and I gradually settled down to life as an English fruit farmer.

Once the land had been replanted, and with the acreage so small, income had to be augmented by interplanting the tree rows with strawberries, gooseberries and market garden crops such as sprouts. The rather decrepit buildings were adapted to house about a thousand laying hens on deep litter – but this venture was not a great success, and I remember remarking that it was like going on holiday when we finally parted with them all.

Over the years various purchases of neighbouring land increased the size of the farm to some 114 acres, with over two thirds of the land planted with apples, and the balance in strawberries, blackcurrants and other soft fruit crops grown mainly for 'pick your own'. In the past, the running of a fruit farm on this scale would have necessitated the provision of expensive grading and cold storage facilities. However, my decision to become a founder member of the Ledbury Cooperative Society, Wye Fruit Ltd, proved a very sensible one, and indeed, in time, Wye Fruit has become one of the premier top fruit cooperatives in England. I will say no more about apples here except to remark that we were sufficiently successful in growing them to be able to send our daughter and two sons away to school – the boys, of course, to Bromsgrove. As apples have now lost a great deal of their profitability, strawberries have become king, and indeed this year – 1997 – we are growing over 55 acres of strawberries, much on rented land and all destined for supermarkets. To pick the quantity of fruit from such an acreage during the conventional months of June and July would have presented almost insuperable problems, and so every measure possible is taken to spread the crop as evenly as possible between May and October. This has required the employment of some very expensive techniques such as planting into polythene beds, trickle irrigation, floating mulches and polythene tunnels. Three lakes have been excavated and a borehole drilled to provide the

Withers Farm House

179

extra water requirements needed. During the summer months up to 80 foreign students are employed, and they are housed on a camp-site of mobile homes. At peak harvesting times, however, additional local casual labour is still required.

Approaching the 1980s, and with the farm well established and the children's education completed, our thoughts turned to seeing something more of the world. My earlier voyages on the Elder Dempster lines and the troopships had given me a great liking for seaboard travel, and had caused me to hanker after seeing something more of foreign climes. My year in Trinidad had in particular attracted me towards the islands of the West Indies. An opportunity in 1979 to travel on a Geest Banana Boat proved to be 'just what the doctor ordered', and this set in train a habit that persisted for the next ten years or more.

Perhaps at the risk of over-emphasising the subject, but wishing to give recognition of a form of travel no longer with us, I include here in full an article I wrote about the Geest Banana Boats:

The Banana Boats

For many years a gleaming white banana ship sailed out of the Bristol Channel each week bound for the Caribbean. These ships were owned by the firm of Geest and normally carried a quota of twelve passengers. The company was originally established by the Dutch family Van Geest, and in competition with Fyffes, gained themselves a big name in the banana industry, and particularly in the West Indies.

Geest supported a thriving cooperatively run banana industry in the Windward Islands, and succeeded in protecting its members from competition from the more cheaply-producing plantations in South America. When, however, in 1995 Geest ceased to trade in bananas, it came as a great shock to the growers, and seemed like the end of an era to the many devoted passengers.

Altogether my wife and I made nine voyages on these banana

boats, and it was only after I had reached the forbidden age of seventy five that I was not allowed to travel any more. It is a rule that cargo boats that carry more than twelve passengers are obliged to carry a doctor. While, for a year or two only, departure was switched to Avonmouth, the traditional home port had always been Barry in South Wales. A typical round trip would normally take about twenty three days. That would be about eight days to reach the first stop of Bridgetown, Barbados, then a week among the islands discharging cargo and loading bananas, and then the homeward run of, again, about a week.

On the voyage out, conditions would gradually warm up, and when the mid-morning beef tea was replaced with ice cream, we knew we were approaching the tropics. Once the first flying fish were sighted and the Southern Cross became visible in the night sky, we knew we really were there. The only sign of land on the voyage would be a glimpse of the Azores as we sailed past. Only once were we privileged to sail close to the island of Pico with its spectacular volcano with a ring of cloud just below the summit.

After a stay of two days in Bridgetown, we would sail on to the other islands, usually St Lucia, St Vincent, Dominica, and the one I always thought the loveliest of all, Grenada. While the ship's company busied themselves, we passengers would have seven or eight full days ashore, either relaxing on the beaches, or exploring by taxi the many features that made each island so different from the others. Just to mention a highlight of each – the spectacular peaks on St Lucia known as the Pitons, the two-mile-long Grande Anse beach on Grenada, the roar of the surf on the black sandy shores of St Vincent, the tropical rain forest that still covers much of Dominica, and rum punches at the Sandy Lane Hotel on Barbados. We had, I am sure, an advantage over the big cruise ships that we often encountered among the islands. Their visit to an island might be for a few hours only, while we could stay ashore all day, only returning to our floating hotel in time for dinner.

Of course, as on all other cargo boats, the ship's itinerary could be altered at short notice, though usually such changes were welcome. For example, in 1981, a hurricane had so reduced supplies of bananas on the islands that we were obliged to sail on to Columbia in South America to make up our quota. Here we anchored for several days at Turbo, a mile or two offshore. We were with a number of other banana boats busily loading from lighters. Geest of course arranged a visit ashore, but the approach was somewhat alarming as the small launch had to negotiate a rather choppy sea and dodge large tree trunks that were emerging from an adjacent river mouth. We returned drenched! That particular voyage was extended to thirty-three days.

Some people might wonder how passengers could exist on such a small ship without getting bored. We never found this to be a problem. While the passengers did indeed come from a variety of backgrounds, they did have one thing on common – a love of sea travel. Provided one was prepared to meet in the bar twice a day, the rest of the time passed quickly enough snoozing or reading on the deck. Meals were of course excellent and, believe it or not, it was customary to dress for dinner. Then we would usually be joined by the captain and the more senior ship's officers.

Attendance at the bar was no hardship as drinks were strictly duty free. A large whisky or gin would cost no more that eight pence! Indeed, it was rather unpopular to order a gin and tonic instead of a pink gin as the tonic would cost more than the gin!

After dinner, entertainment would include films, bingo, quizzes, etc.

It might be mentioned that the Geest ships were not equipped with stabilisers and, to put it mildly, were capable of rolling quite a lot in heavy weather. Despite this, most passengers soon developed their sea legs. Our trips were usually made in the late English winter or early spring. Then it was the high season in the West Indies with little rain and lower humidity. The ships' stewards were mainly recruited in South Wales. I have already mentioned that my favourite island was Grenada. Stewards also liked to be asked which was their favourite. This enabled them to reply with a twinkle in the eye – Barry Island.

This short account of the Geest Banana Boats can only provide nostalgic memories. I am afraid their like will not be seen again.

I will also mention another unorthodox Geest trip in 1984. Then the *Geest Bay* was in dry dock at Lisbon having suffered damage to the hull during a storm in the Atlantic, and this involved the company in flying us out to Lisbon to join the ship there. Geest generously put us up in a nice hotel for three nights, laying on transport to visit various points of interest. Indeed, I afterwards realised that I had unnecessarily bought drinks at the bar as the company would have paid!

While it was about the same distance from Lisbon to the West Indies as it would have been from Barry, we found that our arrival there coincided with that of another Geest ship, so we passengers were delighted to find that we were to spend an extra week among the islands waiting for a full cargo. Indeed, the round trip was one of 31 days instead of the normal 23 days.

Latter-day cruises were not confined to the Geest Line and we travelled several times on such ships as the *QE2*, the *Canberra*, and the *Black Watch* of the Olsen Line. Apart from exploring the Mediterranean and the Canaries, we visited New York and Florida and 'collected' these other West Indies islands – Puerto Rico, St John and St Thomas in the American Virgin islands, Antigua, St Kitts, Martinique, and Bermuda which is, of course, not in the Caribbean. No visit to Madeira could be made without a visit to the famous Reid's Hotel.

There has been one other activity which has kept us in touch with West African days – our continued membership of the 2nd West African Infantry Brigade Association. We have usually attended the annual lunch, which has latterly been held at the Victory Club off Marble Arch. While by 1997 the assembly was getting a 'little long in the tooth' and numbers had dropped to the thirties, the spirit remains just as keen, and groundnut stew has for some years appeared on the menu.

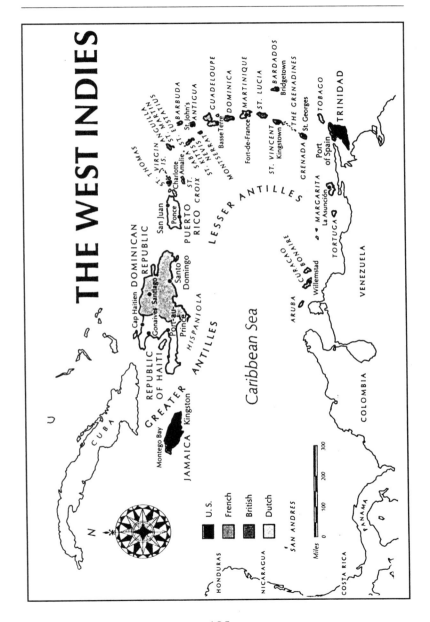

THE WEST INDIES

34

More of the West Indies

As an afterthought, I include a few more impressions of the six islands that were regularly visited by the Geest banana boats:

Antigua

It was only latterly that Geest took in Antigua together with Barbados as an additional starter destination for cargo disposal. Antigua, of course, does not grow bananas and we landed there only twice. On the first occasion we took in the usual tourist spots – Nelson's Dockyard, English Harbour, Shirley Heights and Clarence House, the Governor's residence. On the second visit we spent the day on the beach at the Hawkesbill Hotel, some ten miles out of St Johns, the capital. This was very annoying for the resident travel tout who had come aboard, as it required the hiring of a taxi outside his jurisdiction! I would like to mention here that we always found the West Indian taxi drivers most accommodating and helpful. They would always drive you to your chosen destination at an agreed price, and return again in the evening to pick you up again at no extra charge. You could always rely on them coming back as payment was not usually made until the end of the day.

Banana Boat – The Geest Star

Barbados

Barbados should be pronounced 'Barbadus', not 'Barbadoes' or 'Barbadoss'. When I first landed in Barbados in 1947, visiting ships had to lie offshore. Nowadays there is a splendid harbour that allows even the largest cruise ships to tie up, and as the passengers come ashore they are serenaded by calypso-playing steel bands. The busy capital of Bridgetown boasts a number of very large stores that sell anything and everything, and bear the name of such prominent businessmen as Cave Shepherd, Da Costa and C. F. Harrison & Co. We once visited Bridgetown in late November, and it seemed a little strange then to find these emporiums blaring out all the well-known Christmas carols! We always called at a particular record shop in the town to purchase the latest calypso discs of the island's premier band, the Merrimen.

Apart from all the lovely beaches along the west coast, sights worth visiting on Barbados included Sam Lord's castle on the Atlantic side. While this is now a hotel, it is alleged to be the

187

former home of a notorious buccaneer who lured ships on to the reef by hanging lighted lanterns on the coconut palms. He was later to be hanged, and the tale has become the subject of a famous calypso. We have mentioned Andromeda gardens and the Bannochies elsewhere in the book, but whenever we went on the island we usually ended up at Sandy Lane Hotel. As the years went by, Sandy Lane became more and more exclusive and entry more difficult unless one partook of a large lunch. This always seemed rather unnecessary with an equally large dinner in prospect on the ship in the evening. While by law Barbados hotels were not allowed to ban the public from the beach, Sandy Lane's uniformed attendants effectively patrolled the beach chairs. As one can imagine, there were ways of getting over this, and on our last visit (on the *Canberra*, incidentally) the production of a Forte Gold card made us instant VIPs! Every day we watched a garishly-decorated schooner, the *Jolly Roger*, sailing along the shores. Needless to say we didn't sign on. The passengers were of the younger element who we heard got rather uproarious on unlimited free rum.

St Lucia

An attractive island with the capital Castries. In the town we liked to visit 'Rain', a bar with its theme based on Somerset Maugham's short story of that name, though truth to tell his tale took place in the Pacific. At night we sometimes attended the Green Parrot, a restaurant/nightclub not far from the ship's berth. Among the beach resorts we liked Halcyon Days and, on the northern tip of the island, the German-owned hotel, Steigenburgers Cariblue. After all we had previously heard, we were not surprised to encounter there some rather arrogant Germans competing for the beach chairs!

All visitors to St Lucia must go to Soufrière and the drive-in volcano which is dominated by the spectacular Pitons – two towering spires of lava, both standing over 2,500 feet in height. The Geest ships sail quite close to them when approaching the island. Once, on the way to Soufrière, we were astonished to encounter an elephant being paraded round the village square, surrounded by children. Later we learnt that it had been brought from England on a Geest ship by Colin Tennant. As, no doubt, the only elephant in the Caribbean, I must confess to feeling rather sorry for it, but probably it found the climate congenial! English people liked to go to Bagshaw's, a European-run shop between Castries and the Le Tok Hotel, specialising in locally-designed shirts, linen goods, table mats, etc. The owner rather surprised me by saying that he did not take credit cards but would trustingly accept personal cheques. I expect they are more up-to-date nowadays.

My agriculture connections led to us being entertained by the McKays, the husband being employed by the Windward Islands Banana Association. He took us on one particularly interesting drive in his Land Rover across the centre of the island, and then down the comparatively little-known eastern road to Vieux Fort on the most southern tip. On the way we were able to inspect a number of banana plantations and packing stations. I was rather intrigued when McKay pointed out a largish area of now scrubby land which, he said, in the past had carried crops of sugar cane. Apparently the presence of the extremely deadly snake, the Fer de Lance (Trigonocephalus Lanceolatus), had driven out the cane cutters. An interesting tale from Patrick Leigh Fermor's book, *The Traveller's Tree*, recounts how at the end of the last century a party of sailors attempted to scale one of the Pitons, but the attempt failed as, one by one, the climbers fell at various points on the way to the summit from the bite of deadly Trigoncephale. Generally speaking, however, venomous snakes are absent from West Indian islands.

We were able to rejoin the ship at Vieux Fort, which was occasionally used by Geest as an additional loading port. With no power-loading facilities available there, however, the bananas had to be carried on to the ship by queues of mammies. While to an old African hand like myself there seemed nothing very unusual about this, some of the other passengers thought this to be a rather degrading practice. However, I was later informed that the ladies were very jealous of this 'perk' and would on no account let the men take it over!

St Vincent

This volcanic island lacks the white sandy beaches and, consequently, the larger hotels found on some of the other islands. The capital, Kingstown, is fairly small but very clean. In the town Barbara liked a very nice dress shop which produced spectacularly designed clothes and dresses using the batik method of colouring fabrics. Close to where the ship tied up was quite a comprehensive bookshop, the only one that I ever discovered in the Caribbean. Also close to Kingstown were the well-kept botanical gardens which were said to be the oldest in the western hemisphere, and founded as long ago as 1765. Self-appointed guides were eager to point out the 'very' bread fruit tree raised from the original nut brought from the Pacific by Captain Bligh himself. Apart from bananas, St Vincent grows a wide assortment of food crops on its rich volcanic soils, and has always been the world's largest producer of arrowroot. It is unfortunate for them that arrowroot is no longer the popular commodity it once was.

We eventually found a very pleasant place to spend the day when on St Vincent. This was a very small 'hotel' at the end of a very rough road a few miles out of Kingstown called Rauacou. Rauacou consisted of a small open-sided dining room, a small swimming pool and a sitting-out stoep which immediately overlooked the coconut palms and black sandy beach below, on to which a continual series of huge waves thundered. While we seldom saw anybody else there, the resident staff were available to cook us an excellent curry, and there was of course ample beer and rum available. This must be real honesty – a maid brought Barbara a bathing costume she had left behind a year before!

There were quite a few chalets dotted around, but these seemed largely unoccupied or the inhabitants kept themselves to themselves. One of the few occupants that we did meet turned out to be, of all people, the landlady of a local pub at Woolhope near Ledbury, the Butcher's Arms. The owner of Rauacou was a Canadian who loved the place, though he did give the impression at the time of our last visit that he would reluctantly have to give the project up and return to Canada. It hardly looked like a money-spinner.

Grenada

St Georges, the capital of Grenada, has one of the prettiest harbours on the Caribbean. Here we would be met by our elected taxi driver who rejoiced in the unusual name of Sweat. Why he was called Sweat we never found out – he did not appear to perspire a lot, nor was he particularly hard working. He seemed very popular on the island, and people, particularly the children, liked to wave to him as we passed. On arrival for our usual two-days' stay, Sweat would be waiting ready to take us to wherever we wanted to go. Sweat's taxis, like many other in the West Indies, were usually a bit dilapidated, but as they were no doubt bought on the 'never never' system, it might have been difficult at times for the owners to keep up the instalments. On the other hand, our taxi driver in St Vincent, Bob, had a very posh taxi with notices in front and back seats warning about smoking and slamming doors.

Up to the time of our last visit – 1989 – not much progress had been made in establishing new large hotels on the picturesque Grande Anse beach. This was probably partly due to the Cuban invasion. The Cubans, however, did appear to keep themselves very much in the background, and ordinary tourists like ourselves would hardly know they were there; except perhaps you would not be allowed anywhere near the airport, which was being enlarged to an extent hardly necessary for such a small island. Indeed, it seemed over-reaction when the Americans organised a full-scale military invasion. Rumours, however, must have abounded, and Sweat had amusing tales to tell us, particularly when some of Grenada's leading politicians had been incarcerated in the gaol which was set right in the centre of the town.

Our favourite hotels, both small, were the Spice Islands on the Grande Anse, and the Calabash, which was set in a secluded bay at the south of the island. These hotels consisted of the usual open dining complex covered with climbing tropical plants, and with individual chalets in the grounds. The Calabash's barman made outstandingly good rum punches, and the lobster thermidor was irresistible. Spice Islands had, of course, the better bathing, while the Calabash's beach had the disadvantage of a lot of underwater weed which you noticed only when you entered the sea. Despite this, it was wonderfully peaceful sitting under the coconut palms at the Calabash.

Dominica

When our ship was approaching Dominica for the first time, a lady passenger remarked that in her opinion it was not worth going ashore there. I think she had in mind the lack of sandy beaches and other amenities, and she also had the impression that the natives were unfriendly. How wrong she was! It was perhaps true that Roseau, the capital, was a bit of a shanty town with few good shops or hotels. However, one small hotel on the outskirts, the Anchorage, produced a very acceptable drink, rum and coconut water, which I had not encountered anywhere else, and towards the end of our visits, quite a well-run hotel was opened on a high spot in the town with the rather grand name of Reigate Hall.

Dominica is a fantastic island with a spine of steep hillsides separated by rugged valleys mostly clothed with extravagant rain forest. It has always been said that there are as many rivers in Dominica as there are days of the year, and I wouldn't be surprised if the annual rainfall in the higher mountains might also approach this figure in inches. The highest mountain, by the way, is Morne Diablotin (Devil Mountain) with an altitude of over 4,500 feet. I encountered an old colleague of mine from Wye days named Hipkin who had lived in Dominica with his wife for a long time, and had a grapefruit plantation. He gave us lunch at his home, Springfields Plantation, some eight miles from Roseau. He was always going to give us a meal of 'mountain chicken' (large frogs found in the forest) but he never got round to it.

Our first visit to Dominica was in November 1979, only three months after Hurricane David had devastated the island (actually on August 29th). There had been almost 100% damage to banana plantations, and we saw much structural damage to bungalows on high ground overlooking Roseau. What struck me very forcibly was the sight of forest trees with their tops a mass of dead wood. On our next visit things were normal again. How quickly things can change in the tropics.

In Roseau we became friends of a ship's pilot with the name of Hawkins Labesse. Using his own car, he was quite prepared to taxi for us. He always got us back to the ship on time as it couldn't sail without him! The most interesting trip on which Hawkins took us was one through the centre of the island, ending up at Portsmouth, the second town of Dominica, from where the Geest line loaded bananas by lighter before sailing for England in the evening. On the way we halted to walk to the Emerald Pool, where a waterfall tumbled through a tangle of lianas into brilliant, clear deep water. I was not so much impressed by the Emerald Pool, however, as to hear for the first time the call of a bird, the Mountain Whistler, the Siffleur Montagne. The following paragraph, taken from *The Traveller's Tree*, is, in my opinion, beautifully descriptive:

'The only bird we heard all day was the Siffleur Montagne which piped long lugubrious sounds, usually on one note, but occasionally on two, and every few minutes: a noise so melancholy that it seemed the perfect emanation of these sad and beautiful forests. It haunts the high woods of Dominica and nowhere else in the world.'

Epilogue

While our West African days are now nearly forty years ago, it seems like only yesterday. Since then we have often been asked how we have managed to survive without all those dutiful servants. Perhaps surprisingly, though we may have missed them personally, we have managed quite well without them. Barbara, apart from bringing up three children, has efficiently tackled all household duties, and I have proved quite capable of 'passing drinks' without assistance! Perhaps only recently, on returning from the supermarket with all those bags of shopping, I have thought how nice it would be to have a 'boy' to unload the car for us. Signs of old age, I must suppose.

In comparing West Africa with the United Kingdom, I have come to the conclusion that there is one distinct difference, though a simple one. It concerns the presence or otherwise of the television set. In the old colonial days distractions were few, and outside the normal demands of work and social activities, one was able to fit in as much reading as one would like. In this country nowadays there are too many distractions. Newspapers get larger and larger, I follow too many day-to-day sporting events, I take too many magazines, and these factors, together with the demands of the radio and the 'box', give me too little time for reading.

George, our son, has now moved into the farmhouse, swapping

with us his newly-built bungalow scenically placed among the orchards. However, even at the age of eighty one, I am by no means completely retired, and am responsible for looking after certain of the farm's accounts and records, though the office there is now highly computerised. It does indeed seem a little reminiscent of Gold Coast days, however, to have my own individual 'out' tray in George's office, though the label on it says DAD and not ADA (Assistant Director of Agriculture). Apart from this I like to carry out some leisurely pruning during the winter months.

Barbara keeps herself busy with her piano, collecting antiques, gardening and taking an interest in the progress of our eight grandchildren. With cruising now seemingly a thing of the past, I try to keep in touch with the tropics by growing exotic plants in the conservatory, and these now include 'Petrea Volubilis' of Kpeve fame. The real Petrea is now married and lives in Nottingham, but continues with her nursing career. Jonathan is also married and works for W. H. Smith in the north of England. My sister Hilary who worked for the BBC for most of her life now lives in Bristol. My father, many years a headmaster, died in 1960, and my mother, in 1984 at the grand old age of 101. Ross Granny, as she was known to the children, wrote a book on Herefordshire speech, was an expert on local folklore and a great philatelist. In 1954 she was one of the first three women to be admitted as members of the Woolhope Club, hitherto an all-male preserve. Not long afterwards she was appointed as the first lady president. I should perhaps explain that the Woolhope Club was first established in 1851 as a naturalists' field club. It now produces very learned 'transactions', the columns of which are perhaps directed rather more to subjects of an archaeological nature than to natural history.

Bibliography

Tropical Planting and Gardening	Macmillan	1935
The Fall of Italian East Africa	Rosenthal	1941
It's a Long Way to Addis	Birkby	1942
Imperial Commonwealth	Lord Elton	1945
Abyssinian Patchwork	Gandar Dower	1949
Last Chance in Africa	Negley Farson	1950
The African Giant	Stuart Cloete	1956
Abyssinian Adventure	McDonald	1957
The History of the Royal West African Frontier Force	Hayward & Clarke	1964
The Fall of the British Empire	Cross	1968
Volta – Man's Greatest Lake	Moxon	1969
The Two Thousand Mile War	Croskill	1980
Desert, Jungle & Dale	Van Straubenzee	1991
The Scramble for Africa	Pakenham	1991
Dual Mandate in Tropical Africa	Lord Lugard	1922
The Birds of West and Equatorial Africa (2 volumes)	David Bannerman	1953

The West Indies

Touch the Happy Isles	Quentin Crewe	1987
Budget Caribbean	Fodor	1979

The Traveller's Tree	Leigh Fermor	1950
Isles of the Caribbean	Nat. Geographic	1980
The Sunlit Caribbean	Alec Waugh	1948